WHY ARE YOU BEING EDUCATED?

TALKS AT INDIAN UNIVERSITIES

J KRISHNAMURTI

KRISHNAMURTI FOUNDATION INDIA

Published, with permission, by

Krishnamurti Foundation India
Vasanta Vihar, 124, Greenways Road
Chennai - 600 028.
E-mail: publications@kfionline.org
Website: www.jkrishnamurti.in

First edition 2002
Revised, second edition 2014
Reprinted 2018, 2019, 2022, 2025

ISBN: 978-81-87326-39-7

Cover design: Vivek Raju

Printed by

VST Associated Graphics
7, Kamarajar Salai
Thanthai Periyar Nagar
Chennai - 600 087

Is it not the very essence of ignorance when we depend on others for this inward look, this inward understanding, inward observation of the extraordinary processes that go on? To depend on the experts to tell us what to think about ourselves and how to look at ourselves through the philosopher's eyes, or through the eyes of the guru, or those of any of the religious leaders throughout the world—is that not ignorance?

***

And if you are a student, what is your future? Just to pass some examination, get a job, and fall into the trap which the past generation has created, get married, have a little house with a wife and children? And to fight, struggle, be thoroughly discontented, miserable? Is that what is going to happen? That will inevitably happen, though you may be a technocrat with a good salary, a good position, and full of your own importance.

Contents

Introduction

This book consists of six talks that J. Krishnamurti gave at Indian universities and the Indian Institutes of Technology between 1969 and 1984.

Krishnamurti's association with universities goes back to the year 1922 when he visited the Berkeley University. The place made such a deep impact on him that he began to dream of creating in India a similar academic institution. In 1925 Mrs Annie Besant, president of the Theosophical Society, decided to build a World University in India, possibly close to Krishnamurti's birthplace, Madanapalle in Andhra Pradesh. That he shared her vision is evident from the 'Editorial Notes' he wrote for *The Herald of the Star* in April 1925: 'What has absorbed most of my thoughts and time since I got to India is a scheme for the founding of a new International University at Madanapalle in South India. Such an idea has long been a dream of mine, and that dream is now going to be realized.'

Though Krishnamurti's dream did not take shape, his passion for education remained vital throughout his life, resulting in the founding of four schools in India and two abroad.

In the 1920s Krishnamurti addressed teachers and students at the Theosophical College in Adyar, Madras, and Vijayawada in Andhra Pradesh. In 1930 he gave a talk at the Boys College in Tiruchi, Tamil Nadu. Addressing students of the D. J. Sind College in Karachi on 15 February 1933, he begins on a characteristic note:

'I have never passed a single examination. I have sat for three examinations, but you know when you go to the Examination Hall, how everything turns blank. Probably you have not felt like that, but I did, so I tried three times, and three times I successfully failed!' However, he makes due amends for such an opening by seeking the forgiveness of the 'Principal, the Professors, and yourselves'.

Krishnamurti's first significant address to students is to be found in the series of three talks he gave in 1954 at the Benares Hindu University. Towards the late 1960s and early 1970s, when the campuses in the West were in revolt, he gave talks at the University of Puerto Rico, the Claremont Colleges, California, and the New School for Social Research, New York. This was followed by talks at Brandeis, Berkeley, Stanford, and Santa Cruz, which can be found in the two volumes, *You are the World* and *Talks with American Students.*

During the same period, Krishnamurti addressed students in India too. In the six talks in this volume, his chief concern is to awaken students—and the teachers too—to the fact that the pursuit of knowledge does not liberate man from ignorance. While knowledge, especially technological knowledge, is indispensable, it also creates the illusion that we have the intelligence to meet the challenges of life. This illusion makes us neglect the vast and subtle field of the human psyche, the field of human relationship. All this, he declares, is the essence of ignorance.

However, even while trying to shake the students out of their complacency, Krishnamurti also holds before them the possibility of a life in which there can be both meaning and beauty, responsibility as well as freedom. 'If I were a student, I think I would ask that—how to live a very simple life, without conflict, how to live completely, richly, and fully, without any contradiction, so that life does not become a battlefield. Then I would also ask, 'Is there something beyond all this? Is there something that man in the past has always sought?'

For Krishnamurti, right education cannot be based on academic blueprints and programmes. On the contrary, learning for him is synonymous with learning about oneself; it is not the mere pursuit of knowledge but an exploration into the world within. This vision comes through clearly in these talks, which therefore have significance not just for the young but also for parents, teachers, and all those interested in the deeper issues of human existence.

K.K.

The crisis in the technological and human world

TALK AT THE BENARES HINDU UNIVERSITY, 1969

So what is necessary is a total mutation, a total transformation, of the whole structure and nature of the brain and of the mind also, because the crisis is so vast, so complex, not only in the technological world but also in the human world, in the world of daily living. It demands a new mind, a new heart...

Perhaps, after I talk a little, you would be good enough to ask questions, and thus we shall be able to communicate with each other more freely.

I think it must be fairly obvious to most people that violence is spreading throughout the world, every form of violence: rioting, wars, hatred of one group towards another. In America you see race riots and students' revolts; in Europe it takes a different form. And in India you probably know what is going on much better than I do. So one of the great problems is why man lives in violence. Why does he perpetuate violence? The intellectuals have given many explanations: over-population, modern social life, people living cooped up in cities where they have no space at all, technological development that cultivates only a part of the human being, and so on. Scientists have experimented with putting rats in a very narrow space and found that the rats become disoriented and destroy each other because they have no space to live. There have also been other explanations: that society is undergoing a tremendous change and so on. Religions, education, and science have completely failed and have not brought about peace between man and man. On the contrary, society is becoming more and more complex; more and more laws are being passed, and so there are those who say there must be a bigger, nobler, wider, and more authoritarian leadership. There is the communist world with its authority, with its dictatorship, and that too has not solved the problem. If there is any kind of free expression, people are put into an asylum and their card, or whatever it is, is taken away. So, that is what is going on in the world.

How is this violence to be stopped? This country has for many years preached non-violence as an idea, but I am afraid the ideal hasn't been of any value at all because people are just as violent as anywhere else, as has been shown in the students' revolt in this university; in the other cities also there have been riots. This seems to be the most prevalent expression of human relationship: if nothing works, let us burn the other person or destroy him through war, which is caused by divisions as races, nationalities, and so on.

So, seeing all this objectively, not as a philosopher or an intellectual, not as a Hindu or a Muslim or a Buddhist or even as a scientist, seeing all this chaos and misery that is going on in the world, one asks if this stream of violence can ever be stopped. Will a new philosophy, a new leader, a new religion, a new political party put an end to this devastating, destructive relationship between man and man?

No philosophy, no organized religion, no leader can possibly change the human mind; and we are concerned with the human mind, the mind that has been conditioned, shaped, moulded for millions of years to be violent, to create antagonism, to live in enmity, to be in conflict, and to be at war. I think this is a fact most people do accept. Then, seeing this extraordinary phenomenon, this crisis, what is a human being to do? That is, you and I, what are we to do, not about a particular form of violence either in this country or in Europe, America or Russia, but about violence as a whole? The particular form of violence must be understood in the context of the whole of violence. That is, it is no good tackling one form of violence: the student revolt, or the riots, or war, or the class differences such as the white and the black, or the communist ideal opposed to the socialist and the capitalist ideals. I think this phenomenon of violence must be approached from the point of view of the total violence of man. Why is he violent, violent in all his relationships, violent sexually? Why is there this violence which denies security for the whole of humanity?

Is it at all within the reach of man that he can live at peace with his neighbour? I do not know if you have asked yourself the question whether one can live in this world—not as an idea but actually, not theoretically but factually—without withdrawing into a monastery or putting on the *sannyasi* robe, whether one can live without conflict. If you do ask this question seriously, with great attention and care, what will be your answer? Why is there in man psychological, inward, violence, which expresses itself outwardly—socially, economically, racially? I think this is really a very important question to ask. Why has man, who has lived for millions of years and who has inherited this violence from the animal, not been able to find a way of life, a daily existence, in which there is no conflict whatsoever? Conflict is contradiction within oneself, the fragmentation of the whole structure of our being, of our mind and heart, broken up, divided. And where there is division, separation in any form, there must be violence. If a human being within himself keeps life in departments—the business life, the religious life, the social life, the family life, the national life, and so on—where there is such a division, which is a contradiction in himself, there must be not only violence but this dualistic existence. And out of this arises the extraordinary importance he has given to sex, which has now become another form of violence.

It is also violence when we torture ourselves to fit into a particular pattern established by society, by religions, when we condemn ourselves, or discipline ourselves to conform to a pattern. The word *discipline* means to learn, not to conform, not to obey, not to imitate, but to learn, and a mind that is learning and a heart that is looking, observing, is not in conflict. Conflict arises only when there is accumulation of knowledge as opposed to learning—knowledge as the Hindu or the Muslim, the educated or the uneducated. This division must inevitably breed conflict. So why is it that socially, that is in is the relationship between man and man, sexually and religiously, why is it that we have come to a period, to a crisis, when the response to the challenge is always in terms of violence? I hope I am making myself somewhat clear. There is a tremendous challenge in the world now, a new challenge, a great crisis, and our response to this crisis is to be violent and to give such extraordinary importance to pleasure in every form. Our response to the challenge is according to our conditioning, and our conditioning is based essentially on violence, division, and pleasure. I think this is fairly obvious. Tradition in this country plays an extraordinarily destructive part, and we respond to this enormous challenge as a Hindu or a Buddhist or a Muslim or as a student, or this or that. And so when we respond to this challenge inadequately, that is, when we respond traditionally or by seeking pleasure, the very inadequacy of our response breeds great harm, brings about great sorrow, not only to ourselves but also to others.

So what is one to do? Systems have failed. You understand this fact? For instance, communism, which promised so much—no wars, the withering away of the State, and so on—has now become a brutal dictatorship where there is no freedom. And any system—it doesn't matter what it is, sociological or religious—must inevitably fail because the challenge is to create not a new system but a new quality of mind, a different feeling, a different sense of relationship between man and man. So we cannot possibly answer the challenge in terms of the old. Please do understand this very simple fact.

So what is necessary is a total mutation, a total transformation, of the whole structure and nature of the brain and of the mind also, because the crisis is so vast, so complex, not only in the technological world but also in the human world, in the world of our daily living. It demands a new mind, a new heart, and this cannot possibly come about through any system, through any leader, through any kind of organized education. It comes only when human beings—you—are awake, inwardly aware of what is going on within yourself, of how you have divided life into the business, scientific, religious, and family life, aware of this fragmentation of the whole structure of your life. And this fragmentation takes place when there is fear.

You know what fear is, not only the physical fears but the greater, psychological fears. Fear is in relation to something; it doesn't exist by itself. Now, can you be aware of this fear, go into it, understand it? Fear is the expression of the demand to be completely secure, because the brain demands that it be wholly and completely safe, secure, as does the child. Where there is no security, as in the modern society, there is fear. And can this fear be put aside through analysis?

This is really a very serious problem, not just an entertainment; nor is it a philosophical amusement. We are working together. Communication means that: to work, to build, to create together, not for you to merely listen to a few words, agree or disagree, and walk away from here. We are partaking in the understanding of a great problem, which does not need agreement or disagreement. It demands that you pay attention to it, look at it, learn all about it, but you cannot possibly learn all about it if you are afraid. And being afraid you try to escape from it. The escape may be drink, women, sex, the temple, or becoming a *sannyasi*, a monk, but fear is there.

Can this fear be analysed and put aside? Which is what most of the psychologists and analysts are trying to do. Can fear, which is in the human mind and heart, be put aside? Can there be freedom from fear through analysis? In analysis is implied the analyser and the thing analysed. Right? There is the analyser who analyses what he calls fear, looks to the cause of the fear, tries to analyse it, dissect it, open it up. But is the analyser different from the thing he analyses? Or the analyser *is* the analysed? I don't know how you will answer this question.

Probably you have not thought about this at all, though you may be great professors or lecturers or intellectuals. Probably you have not approached the problem this way at all. This may be new to you, so you have to look at it. Is the observer different from the thing he observes? As long as there is this division between the observer and the observed, there must be conflict, and that is the very root of violence. You understand, sir? Human relationship is based on this principle that the observer is different from the thing he observes.

Look at it, sir, you are involved in this. You, the husband or wife, the father or mother, whatever it is, you have your own life of ambition, greed, the pursuit of pleasure, your own competitive life, seeking position, prestige. That is your life, if you are a man. If you are a woman, you have your own life, isolated, different from the husband's. You may sleep together, but the fact is that you are two different entities working within the walls of your own desires, within the walls of your own ambitions and so on. And your relationship is based on the image you have of each other. The relationship is between the images, and so there is division and therefore conflict. That is the real issue—whether this division between man and man as the observer and the observed can ever disappear.

That is, knowledge as experience and memory creates this division between human beings. You have an image of the wife, and the wife has an image of you, built through many years of pleasure, irritation, anger, and so on. These two images have a relationship, not the human beings but the images, which are the memory, the past. So, as long as there is fragmentation in one's life as the observer and the observed, there must be conflict.

You know, sir, when you look at a tree, see the beauty of it, the shape of it, the light on the leaf, see it in the rain, see it in the evening and during the daytime, if you look at it with the memory you have about that tree, if you say that it is a mango or a tamarind or whatever it is, your botanical knowledge about the tree prevents you from looking at it. You become the observer with your knowledge, and the tree is something separate from you. So where there is space between you as the observer and the thing observed, there must be contradiction, and therefore there must be conflict and violence.

So, can this division, which is time and space, disappear? You understand my question? Because we have traced very carefully the process of violence, the way of violence. As long as there is division, separation, space, and time between human beings, the one as the observer and the other as the observed, there must be conflict. When the Hindu, the Muslim, and the Christian, with their images of themselves and with their own beliefs, dogmas, superstitions, observe each other, there is bound to be division and therefore conflict and violence. Right? Now, how is this space to disappear, the space created by thought as the Hindu, as the communist, the space brought about by memory? How is that to disappear so that we meet each other without the image, without the observer as the 'me' and 'you', the 'we' and 'they'? How is this to come to an end totally, completely?

And is love a matter of pleasure, is love desire? You have to answer this question, not look to the speaker, because that is of no value at all. Our social morality, respectability is based on pleasure, and therefore it is utterly immoral. So one has to find out for oneself whether the space between man and man, as the observer and the observed, can be totally dissolved. That is, can we meet as human beings without labels? Because it is only then that we can solve this immense problem of violence among the students, among the priests, among all human beings. Can the mind, which is the product of time, of evolution, of centuries upon centuries of conditioning, break through its conditioning, not in some distant time but immediately? Otherwise your house is burning, and you are not doing anything about it.

Now this is—if I may use the word—meditation, which I hope you will look at, listen to delicately, not with your particular system of meditation, not with your particular idea of what meditation should be, Buddhist, Zen, or Hindu. If you forget all that and listen, you will find that the word *meditation* means to ponder over, to observe, to give attention, to learn. It is not following some stupid system of meditation but making the mind extraordinarily sensitive, alive, not burdened and therefore free. To find the truth of this division between man and man demands that quality of meditation. No book will teach you about it, not the Gita, the Upanishads, the Koran or the Bible, because books are valueless however sacred they are. So you have to go into yourself, but you mustn't dig too deep a hole in yourself, because the more you dig the more you get the same thing: go deeper and deeper and you get caught in its depth. You must touch it lightly because the inquiry into oneself demands great delicacy. You are learning about it. And to learn about something you must not come to it with previous knowledge, saying that you are the Atman or not the Atman, the soul or not the soul; you must come to it with a fresh mind. And that is the beauty of meditation, not all the tricks that one plays with it.

So we have this problem. There is a challenge in the world, not only in this particular part of the world but everywhere, and all challenges are always new. It is not an old challenge, and therefore it demands that you respond to it in an altogether different way, in a new way. If you respond to it in the old terms, you are going to destroy the world. So you have to have a fresh mind, a new mind, a new quality of mind and heart. That can come about only when you observe yourself, when you are aware of yourself, not condemning yourself, but just being aware, watching. And in this watching there are no implications of virtue and therefore no condemnation. Such watching is really the religious mind, and it is only such a mind that can live at peace with itself and bring about peace in the world.

Now, perhaps, you may like to ask questions. First of all, sirs, before you ask questions, find out why you are asking them, whether it is to catch the speaker, to trip him up, to show off your cleverness, to ask for the sake of argument, or whether you are asking to find out what is true objectively and inwardly. Or if you are going to ask questions quoting books, comparing what is being said with what you have already read, let me assure you that the speaker has not read any philosophical or psychological books, the Gita or the Upanishads. Therefore, if you are going to quote and compare, then you will quote and compare for yourself. And to ask the right question is extraordinarily important because the right question can be put only by a mind that has really gone into all this, has really inquired objectively, not as a Hindu or as a philosopher or a professor or a scientist, but as a human being. Therefore the mind is free to inquire, and when such a mind asks a question, it has validity, vitality, significance and depth; but merely to get up and ask, 'Do you mean this or do you mean that?' means nothing. But please don't think that in saying this I am preventing you from asking questions.

Questioner: Does challenge create violence or does violence create the challenge?

Krishnamurti: I don't know. We are going to find out. First of all, why are you asking it? Can violence create the challenge? Please follow this slowly, go into it step by step. Is the challenge creating violence? Now, there is challenge and violence, but why do we divide the two? Why is there this division between what is called challenge and what is called violence, the response? Or is there only challenge and no response? If the response to the challenge is adequate, is there a division at all? The inadequacy to the challenge is there because of human conditioning, his pettiness, his worries, his demand for security, pleasure, and so on. But when the challenge and response go together—that is, when there is only challenge and no response, or when you are responding adequately all the time—then there is no challenge.

The next question is: Why do we have to have challenges at all? You have a challenge only when you are asleep. Right? If you are completely awake, what is the need for challenge? To a man who is awake, watching, observing, learning, what is the need for any challenge at all? It is only the man who is fully asleep or half-asleep who needs to be poked, shoved, pushed, and shaken, and therefore the challenge pushes him to wake up. But to a man who is awake, there is no challenge at all. So the question then is: Why is man asleep?

Do you understand the difference between learning and acquiring knowledge? Learning is one thing and acquiring knowledge is another. Acquiring knowledge is a bondage, and learning is never a bondage. That is, knowledge is always in the past, knowledge implies the past. Scientific knowledge has been gathered for two or three or four hundred years, or a thousand years, and you are adding to it all the time. Something new is discovered and added, and there is this enormous storehouse of scientific knowledge. And having accumulated that knowledge, there is action from that knowledge. But learning is a constant movement without acquiring knowledge. Look, you have had an experience, and you have learnt something about it, from it. That has become your memory, the very brain cells themselves are that memory. You have had an experience, and you have learnt something from it. And having learnt from it, you act. Therefore your action and what you have learnt are two different things. Right? Therefore there is a division.

Put it the other way round: which is, you have an ideal. I don't know why you have it, but most people have ideals. People have ideals, say, of non-violence. That is one of your pet ideals, but your action from the ideal is entirely different. You say, 'I am approximating my action to the ideal.' And so there is always an approximation, a division, and therefore there is conflict. Whereas if you had no ideal, but *only the fact*, then you are learning about the fact, not acting from what you have learnt. You are always living in the active present of that verb 'to learn'. A mind that is learning, a mind that is constantly in movement, constantly watching becomes extraordinarily sensitive, alive, and therefore vitally intelligent. Why does such a mind need a challenge at all? Light doesn't need challenges: it is light. It is only in darkness that there is challenge, the demand for light.

Questioner: I am not able to understand how the observer is also the observed.

Krishnamurti: 'Why do you say the observer is the observed?' Now, if there is fear. is the observer different from the fear? You understand, sir? There is fear. Is that fear different from the one who is observing the fear? Are they not the same? When you are hungry, is the hunger different from the thinker who says he is hungry? Or, are they both the same? Look, when you observe a tree and have the botanical knowledge, like or dislike of that tree, you look at it through the eyes of prejudice. But when you have no prejudice, when you look at it with clear eyes, there is no space between you and the tree. Then your relationship to it is entirely different. Then the tree, the root, the branch, the whole structure of the tree becomes extraordinarily alive, because there is no division, there is no screen as knowledge between you and that.

Now, can you look at your wife or husband that way? Have you ever tried it, to look without the knowledge you have accumulated about her or him, without your prejudice, without like and dislike, without the image that you have? Then, when you so look, do you look with the eyes of love or with the eyes of prejudice?

Questioner: What is the practical way out of this violence in which man lives?

Krishnamurti: The practical way is the way of violence! Don't laugh, please listen to that question. He says, 'Please tell me what is the practical way.' Which means he accepts authority. He doesn't know, so he says, 'Please, for God's sake, tell me what to do, what is the practical way.' And the demand for the practical arises because one is confused oneself and therefore looks to another. That is what you have done for a million years—looking to somebody to tell you what to do, how to breathe, how to meditate, how to live with each other, how to have sex or not to have sex. So you get up now and say, 'Please tell me what to do', which means you are still caught in the pattern of tradition, of authority. Therefore the first thing is to be free from authority. Don't look to another, including the speaker, especially the speaker, because you are very easily influenced.

So, can the mind be free of authority? Which doesn't mean you become rude, violent, and all the rest of it. Understand why, legally and inwardly, you want authority. Because you are afraid, you look to another; you want to be told like a child what to do. And there are millions of people to tell you what to do, all your books, all your gurus tell you what to do. Which means you will never find out for yourself, never learn. And one of the things that is destroying this world is authority.

So the practical way, sir, is to understand why you have authority, why you follow another—the communist, the socialist, or your guru. Why? Because you are frightened, you want to be secure, you don't want to make a mistake. Why not make a mistake and learn? A mind which is afraid seeks authority as a shelter, and where there is shelter there is darkness.

Questioner: [*Inaudible*]

Krishnamurti: 'You speak of love, and I don't know what it means.' Is that it? Right, sir. What does love mean to you, not as an idea, not as a principle, not as a theory, not as a belief, not what the book says; but do you know what it means? You are grown up, married, and have children; do you know what it means? Or the young people, the students, do you know what it means?

Audience: Living in unity.

Krishnamurti: That is an idea, isn't it? Have you unity, actually? Or is it just an idea, an ideal, a theory, a goal, a principle? Therefore brush all that aside, for God's sake; face the fact. Look at it, find out what it means, not what it should be. It is like a hungry man who wants food, not the description of food. But you are not hungry; you are fed on words and therefore you say 'unity'. So let's find out.

What is love? Do you know what it means, what actually it is now? It is associated with sex and pleasure. Right? It is not the love of God, of humanity, of truth; all that is nonsense. That is just a theory, living in a mystical, fallacious, illusory world. But the fact, as it is now in this world, is that when you pick up any magazine, any book, it talks about love, sex, and pleasure. Can you face that fact? No, you are too frightened. Now, if you face the fact, then the question is: Is love pleasure? When you have pleasure, there must be fear with it—that you might lose it. You take pleasure in the belief that there is or there is no God, and you hold on to it. When someone questions that belief, you become afraid and therefore antagonistic. So pleasure must inevitably bring fear with it. That is an obvious fact. So, is love pleasure, fear, pain, jealousy? Don't say no. This is what you call love. If love is not all that, then you must be free of jealousy, envy, possessiveness, domination. Then the thing will be there; you won't have to look for it. But we have dissipated this energy called love through pleasure. So one has to understand pleasure and joy.

Is joy or ecstasy, pleasure? Pleasure has always a motive, a cause, an object which evokes a response.

There is always the one who seeks pleasure from or through something, through a person, position, money, belief, this or that. But is joy, ecstasy, dependent on anything? If it is, it is pleasure. Pleasure has a continuity in time brought about by thought. But joy is not the product of thought. It has no cause, and that is why one has to go into this non-verbally to find out, to learn. And that is the greatest revolution, not all these shoddy little revolutions, economic or social revolutions. The real revolution is the psychological, inward, revolution, so that your mind is free from authority, from fear. And when you understand joy, when there is joy, then you will know what pleasure is. In the greater the lesser is, but if you cling to the lesser, the greater has no value for you.

Sir, love is not thought, love is not jealousy. When the mind is free from fear, from this demand to be eternally secure, free from ambition, greed, envy, and the things of the mind that fill the heart, when the mind and the heart are empty of the things that the mind has brought about through thought, then there is love. You don't have to look for it, you don't have to go out and say, 'I must be loved' or 'I must love.' There is love; it is not yours or mine. And that is the beauty and the holiness of love.

Questioner: How do definitions condition the mind?

Krishnamurti: Does a definition condition the mind? One of the most difficult things is to be free of the word, to be free of the description and remain only with the described. For, most people love definitions, love descriptions, love verbal exchanges. Look, the word *God* has caught you, you are enslaved by that word. That is your conditioning and your definition of what God is. By the definition, by the description you are caught.

That definition, that description, that formula conditions your mind. Therefore one has to be free of the word, because the word is not the thing. The word *door* is not the door. So the mind caught in a description, in a definition, in a formula is always conditioned.

Questioner: This awareness you talk of—what does it mean?

Krishnamurti: First of all, let us say that awareness is not the result of a practice. To practise awareness means watching, being aware of what you are doing, thinking, So awareness is not to be practised—full stop. That is the first thing. Do you accept that?

Questioner: Yes, sir.

Krishnamurti : I don't think you do, sir; I will show you. There are a great many schools throughout the world trying to practise awareness. They say: 'Be aware of how your toe wiggles, be aware of what you are thinking, be aware of how you walk, and so on; watch it, watch it.' That is called awareness. But we say, that is not awareness; it is a part of it but not the whole of it.

What does awareness mean? To be aware? You are aware that I am sitting here. If you are conscious that I am sitting here and that the 'me' who is sitting here on the platform is an image that you have about him—the reputation that he is a great man or a stupid man—it prevents you from being aware. So you are not being aware when there is any form of image-forming. Any interference of thought in observation denies awareness. Because thought is the response of memory, thought is always old, is never free. Therefore, when thought comes and says,

'You must be aware', then it is thought that is aware, but there is no sense of *being* aware. So when awareness is not the product of thought, when it is free from thought, then there is only attention without any compulsion, without any direction. When you attend completely with your whole being, with your mind, your heart, your brain, your nerves, then there is total awareness in which there is no fragmentation as the observer and the observed, the one who is aware and the thing that he is going to be aware of.

27 November 1969

On knowledge and ignorance

FIRST TALK AT THE UNIVERSITY OF BOMBAY, 1969

On the one hand, we cultivate knowledge about nature, about matter, science, and so on, and totally disregard probably the one most important thing in life, which is the structure and nature of our own mind. Surely, that is ignorance.

This is supposed to be a students' meeting, but I see very few students. All the same, I hope you wouldn't mind it if the speaker addresses himself to the students.

One often wonders why one gets educated at all. Is it to acquire knowledge of the things of the world, the various things that are going on in the world, mostly informative—technological, sociological, and economic? That knowledge is obviously necessary. Probably most of us, when we go to college or university, hope to prepare for the coming life—whatever that word may mean—for the life that one has to live every day: acquiring a job, keeping the job, and climbing the ladder of success, if one has the capacity. For that, obviously, knowledge, scientific, economic, or literary, is necessary.

So where do knowledge and ignorance begin? One may have all the technological knowledge about the world, about the atom, about how to build computers, how to go to the moon, and to do all the extraordinary things that man is doing right throughout the world. A fantastic technological advancement, a tremendous revolution is going on, and I think most of us are aware of it. We are becoming more informed, more and more capable of meeting the world, of meeting nature and its storms, of going to the moon and beyond; there the mind is extraordinarily capable. And one asks, what is ignorance? You know what knowledge is—going to college, university, if you are lucky, acquiring all the book knowledge and what the professors and experts can give you along any line: sociology, economics, physics, biology, anthropology, and so on. That we call knowledge. Then what is ignorance? Apparently, we are ignorant people, and therefore we have to acquire knowledge to meet this extraordinarily complex society, to live in this world at all. So we say we must have knowledge, not only to get a better job but also to live in this modern world. That's granted, that's so. I think most of us would agree that this is necessary. Then, what is this thing called ignorance? Or doesn't it at all enter our minds to inquire into what is ignorance? We have acquired knowledge, but apparently we haven't inquired into the whole field of man's ignorance.

What is ignorance? Is it not the utter disregard, the utter neglect of the complicated and extraordinarily subtle, psychological world? Apparently there too we have certain knowledge given by the experts: the philosophers, the psychologists, the analysts, and so on. But again we have acquired knowledge about ourselves through others, through the Gita, the Upanishads, the Koran, the Bible, the Freuds, and the Jungs. They have told man what he is. That is still knowledge—being informed through others about ourselves. Is this knowledge, or is it total ignorance when we cultivate information, when we learn from others what we are, *how* we should think, and *what* we should think? Is it not the very essence of ignorance when we depend on others for this inward look, this inward understanding, inward observation of the extraordinary processes that go on? To depend on the experts to tell us what to think about ourselves and how to look at ourselves through the philosopher's eyes, or through the eyes of the guru, or those of any of the religious leaders throughout the world—is that not ignorance? On the one hand, we cultivate knowledge about nature, about matter, science, and so on, and totally disregard probably the one most important thing in life, which is the structure and nature of our own mind. Surely, that is ignorance. However clever you may be, however erudite and well informed about all current events, however proficient technologically, when you disregard entirely what is going on inside the skin, it is a form of total ignorance. So you have extraordinary knowledge on the one hand and absolute ignorance on the other.

And this ignorance, this lack of comprehension of ourselves, is creating havoc in the world, in spite of all the universities, whether they be the communist universities or the capitalist universities or the universities in this country. This total disregard of what is happening inwardly, psychologically, and this division is producing great disaster, if one observes, if one is at all have of what is going on in the world. The student riots throughout the world are concerned with getting better jobs, with making life more certain in a world that is overpopulated and where everything has become extraordinarily uncertain, insecure; and being incapable of meeting it, we turn to others to be informed about ourselves, to be directed. And this is where conflict, misery begin, when we divide the world into the outer and the inner; when we completely concentrate on the outer and totally disregard the inner; or give all our thought to the inner and totally disregard the outer, seeking the essence and not being concerned with the expression of that essence. So we have these two worlds: the outer and the inner. Similarly, we have divided man into the higher, the soul, the Atman, and the physical organism as two separate states or entities. But if one is aware, one sees that there is a psychosomatic relationship going on constantly—an interrelationship between the body and the mind, and the mind and the body. So the question is not how to bring about a revolution outwardly. There have been revolutions outwardly, which haven't changed man at all—the Communist, the French, and the other forms of revolution which have destroyed millions and millions deliberately to force man to conform to a pattern. They have all utterly failed.

Surely there is only one revolution, this inward revolution, which affects the outer. Not the outer first, then the inner, or the inner first and the outer second: it is one unitary movement. Therefore one cannot be ignorant of or disregard the inner, because the inner demands, the inner urges, appetites, drives, compulsions change the outer—the outer form, the outward expression, the outward morality. So in considering the inner we are not neglecting the outer. We are only saying that without understanding the inner, however much you may change the outer with new laws, new structures of society, new economic, social conditions, you do not solve the problem of the human being. You may bring about a little more order, but that order will inevitably be destroyed by your own inner demands, greed, and fear. So, however erudite you may be, however extraordinarily well-learned you may be, ignorance is that quality of mind that is totally unaware of what is going on inside the skin. So this division that is going on in the world and this total disregard of what is happening within bring about not only social disaster but a total perversion of the human mind. And I think it is very important to inquire into that—to *inquire*, not to be *told* what to inquire into, to observe, not to be told what to observe.

First of all, inquiry demands freedom. If the mind is prejudiced, if it holds on to a certain belief, dogma, hope, and therefore to despair and fear, it is not free to inquire. A mind that is tethered to a certain belief—that there is a soul, an Atman, or that there is no Atman and so on—tethered to a particular conclusion, religious or non-religious, Marxist or Vedantin, cannot inquire. So there must be freedom.

Inwardly you are not free. You may have money, a job that makes you travel all over the world—my particular job has been to go all over the world—but that is not freedom. Freedom is to learn, to inquire, to discover, to find out. And it is not possible to inquire, to learn if there is fear, if there is a compulsive demand or an insistent conditioning. So inquiry demands freedom. Otherwise the scientist cannot look into the microscope and discover; he must be free from all hypotheses. If he looks at things through a microscope with a mind that has a hypothesis, he cannot see what is actually going on. So, to inquire into this whole world of ourselves, absolute freedom is necessary, not relative freedom.

So we need to inquire into what that freedom is which will help us to observe—not what to observe, but the freedom to look. If there is any form of distortion, any twist, not only in the physical eye but also in the inward eye, in the mind, in the heart, then inquiry has no meaning. Isn't that so? If say, 'I am a Hindu' and observe with all my prejudices, superstitions, and conditioning, I cannot see. I will see what I have been told or conditioned to, project that from my background, and see what I *should* see. So freedom is the negation of any distortion.

Freedom is possible only where there is no fear. Fear prevents one from looking. It is like a mind that lives in darkness and is searching for light. Freedom is that movement of the mind and heart when there is no fear of any kind. Right? Our question then is: Is it possible for the mind and the brain and the physical organism to be entirely free of fear? Now, we are going to find out together. You are not going to be told by the speaker what to do, for you to learn by heart and then apply what you have learnt to get rid of fear—that is what we have been doing for millions of years. We are going to find out for ourselves what fear is, study it, learn all about it, go into it, and see if the mind can free itself from fear totally.

There is the organic fear of survival—the bodily fear that demands food, clothes, and shelter; the fear that arises when you meet a snake or danger. And there are many other forms of fear, some of which we shall go into presently. The demand for physical security for the organism to survive—is that fear? You understand? When you meet a physical danger and react to it, is it fear? When you meet a snake or some wild animal and you respond instantly, is the response based on fear? Please, we are inquiring. The speaker is not going to tell you what it is based on; we are learning, we are communicating with each other. The physical organism, with its brain, has been conditioned for millions of years to meet danger. When you see a snake, there is instant response. Is that response based on fear or on intelligence?

Please do inquire into this yourself. Do not wait for a reply from the speaker. If you wait for a reply, then you make the speaker an authority, a professor. We are speaking in a college where the professor is the authority, but I hope you are not going to make the speaker an authority, because authority is the denial of freedom when we are inquiring. So there is no authority, at least as far as we are concerned. And it is a great act of understanding when you put aside all authority in order to find out, to inquire: your mind is already free. And going into the whole question of authority is not what we are concerned with for the moment. But in understanding fear, we will see its relationship to authority.

So we are asking: Is it fear that prompts instant action when you meet danger? Though from the very beginning of time the brain cells and the whole organism have been conditioned to react to danger, the reaction is surely not fear but intelligence. Intelligence demands that you survive; otherwise, you could go and throw yourself under a bus! So intelligence is the awareness of danger and the possibility of destruction, of non-survival. I know this opens up a great many questions, but we will meet those if we begin to understand the nature of fear.

Now we are going to inquire into fear, not only at the conscious level but also at the deeper layers of the mind by following not the words but by observing our own fears. If you are a student, you are frightened of the future, obviously. In an overpopulated country like this, there is the uncertainty about jobs and so on. When there is fear, we cannot possibly inquire, either into the outward structure of society or into the much more subtle, much more intricate field of ourselves. Therefore one must understand, learn, be aware of the whole structure and nature of fear.

Fear is resistance, and resistance implies division. And where there is division there is insecurity, and so there must be fear. Are we going together? We have learnt something new, we have discovered something new—that resistance has different forms, as nationality, as family, as my belief and your belief, my opinion and your opinion, my god and your god, my way of thinking and your way of thinking, my experience opposed to your experience or knowledge. And any conclusion is a resistance. Where there is any form of resistance, it must inevitably bring about fear.

So the mind, in observing, is learning about the nature and structure of fear. Therefore when you are learning about fear, it is your learning, not my learning being given to you. You know, it is one of the most extraordinary things in life that we want to be told what to do, that we are always looking for somebody to guide us. The speaker has nothing to offer, he has no message to give you. He is not telling you what to do or giving you new ideals, new philosophies, or a new set of rules. All he is saying is, 'Observe, look.' And you cannot possibly look, observe, and listen if there is fear.

So there is fear when there is any form of division and resistance. When you use the word *nationalism*, you divide the world. When you separate yourself as a Hindu, a Muslim, a Parsi, and the other man does the same, you are bound to have wars. So any form of isolation, exclusion, will inevitably bring about disaster and fear. So resistance, which is to build a wall round oneself, will inevitably bring fear.

The next inquiry is: Why do the mind and the brain cells resist, divide as 'we' and 'they' and so on? Why? I don't know how we are going to inquire into this, because the mind is divided in itself, as the conscious and the unconscious, as tradition and new knowledge, as mine and yours. And one part, one fragment, of the mind says, 'I must inquire into why this whole division and resistance take place.' You are following all this? We have created resistance, we have resistance: like, dislike, mine, yours and all the rest of it. We have innumerable resistances. Resistance exists because we don't want to be hurt; we want to be secure, and that very resistance creates fear. So the mind, realizing this, asks, 'Why do I divide, why do I resist?'

Now, which part of the brain is asking this question? Is it the one part which has separated itself or the totality of the being that is asking the question? You see the difference? One fragment of the mind which has separated itself from fear says, 'I have understood now that fear comes into being when there is any form of resistance.' That particular part now asks the question, 'Why do I resist?' Is that not a wrong question? How can you answer a fundamental, all-comprehensive question when that question is put by a small segment of the mind? Its answer will always be partial and therefore not true. Therefore, can the segment of the mind ask a question which is all-comprehensive? Or is it only a mind that is not fragmented that can ask this question?

So the inquiry now is not what brings about resistance but whether the mind can look at the totality of fear—the fear of death, fear of being dominated by another, fear of having no security, fear of losing one's life. Will you answer each fear by itself, by one of the fragments of the mind, or will you ask a total question which will have the total answer?

So we are now going to find out, inquire, not into fear but into the nature of a mind that is non-fragmented, so that when it asks a question there will be a total answer. Now, what is the mind and heart that are not fragmented, that have no resistance whatsoever and therefore no fear, and so can look into fear? When we say 'a fragment of the mind', 'a segment', 'a part', what does that mean? Have you ever observed your own mind, observed it, not corrected it, not said it is right or wrong, but just observed it? There are these innumerable divisions in oneself, various desires, various pleasures, fears, sorrows, and there is the pursuit of pleasure and the avoidance of pain, of fear—have you ever observed all this in yourself? If you have, who is the observer? Is he not a fragment of the brain, of the mind, which is observing? That is, a part, a segment, is observing other segments, other broken-up parts. This is really interesting. If one part is observing the other part, its answer will always be partial, and therefore resistance can never be resolved. Therefore fear can never go. So our question is: How does the mind look, observe? Does it observe as a part, a segment, or is the totality of the mind observing?

We are now inquiring into whether the mind can observe without any fragment, without the observer taking part. Is there an observation without the part, the segment, taking action? Which is, observation without the observer. The observer is the fragment, the past. When you observe this microphone, or look at the sunset, the palm tree, or your wife, you are looking through the past, the past being knowledge, information, experience, which is essentially a fragment. And the past must inevitably create resistance. Because you have had fear, you have had pleasure, you say, 'My goodness, will I have more pain tomorrow?' 'Will I have more pleasure tomorrow?' So the past is the observer, is the fragment. And the mind asks, 'Can there be observation without the observer?' This is really an extraordinarily important question. Because if the answer is true, then you have broken down the whole structure of effort, of struggle, of conflict, and therefore of violence.

So to find out, one has to observe the manner of one's seeing in daily life—the look you give to the tree, to your wife or husband, to your professor, to the future. And can you see without the observer? Because when there is an observer, he creates space and time, which is a resistance. Therefore the very essence of conflict is this division between the observer and the observed. And that is our conditioning. We have been so brought up from childhood. That has been our conditioning for thousands of years—the higher self and the lower self, the Atman and the physical, God and devil, the good and the bad, social morality and its immorality, and so on. So, can the 'I', that is the heart, the mind, the brain cells, the physical organism itself observe without projecting the implications, the associations of the past?

You know, those who take drugs, especially LSD, have told us that when they take this particular form of chemical, the space between the observer and the observed disappears, and therefore there is an immediate relationship, an immediate contact, a direct contact, a direct relationship. You see things as you have never seen anything before in your life. I know a man who takes this drug and goes to the museums to see the pictures there. And the colours and proportions, the depth, the shade and the light he sees is something incredible. That is caused by a chemical reaction; therefore you depend on the drug, and you have to take more of it, like an alcoholic. You have to take it all the time in order to see the marvels of the world.

Now, what we are saying is: Without the drug, without the chemical process—which takes place also when you fast, making your body extraordinarily sensitive—without doing any of these tricks, can you see, observe without the observer? Then you will see the most extraordinary thing taking place, something fantastically different from what happens through the drug. Because then it is not an induced thing, not a cultivated thing, but an actual, experiential, pragmatic reality. Which means there is no separation of time and distance and, therefore, no effort. Life then is something entirely different. If you make a mistake, you correct it immediately. If there is a little conflict, you watch it and eliminate it; there is an elimination of it through observation because there is no observer. Therefore there is immediate action.

So the mind observes fear without the observer. It is only then that you can put the total question. And the total answer, obviously, is, 'There is no fear', which is not a logical conclusion but an actual fact. Look, sirs, one is afraid of death. I don't know why, but one is. Now, how are you going to answer that question? Please do watch it, do inquire into it freely, not asking whether there is reincarnation or a permanent soul and all the rest of that. Those are all traditional, worn-out answers that don't really answer anything. Because if you really believe in reincarnation, it means you must live at the supreme height now; otherwise, you will pay for it next life. Right? But you don't; you believe in reincarnation and yet you live any old way. So, that belief has no validity at all. What has validity is your living, not what happens tomorrow.

Now, one is afraid of death. You know death, the ending of the physical organism, the death of all that you have cherished, held dear; you know what is implied by death. How does the mind look at this problem? Does it resist it? Is it afraid of it? Is there hope in an idea of reincarnation or a future life, or of sitting next to God in a cloud, and all the rest of it? Or does the mind observe without the observer? If you do observe without the observer, is there death? There is organic death. But is there then such a thing called death which so dominates our lives? Find out, not through drugs, but through this whole observation of the structure of fear. Find out what is observation, what is fear, what is resistance, become aware of resistance, aware of not only the conscious fears but also of the unconscious fears. But we haven't the time to go into that now.

So we come back to the fundamental question: what is ignorance? Ignorance is this unawareness of the whole structure and nature of the mind, the brain, and all its movement; that is the very essence of ignorance. You learn from books and from your professors, pass examinations, get a few degrees and get a job—*that is nothing*. That is necessary in this mad world. But to be totally unaware of this extraordinary inward movement, the beauty, the subtlety, the quickness of this movement, to be unconscious of it, to be unaware of it is not only ignorance, but it brings about destruction.

Perhaps, if you are not bored or tired, you might like to ask questions. But before you ask questions, find out why you ask, because if you could answer the 'why', for what reasons you are asking, you would have found the answer for yourselves. We ask a question for somebody else to tell us the answer and either agree or disagree with that answer. So then you are really not asking a question at all; you are just offering an opinion in the form of a question. And opinion is not truth. Dialectically, opinion does not show what truth is. So if you go into this whole question of asking questions, it is quite an extraordinary thing.

Why do we ask a question? Who is going to answer? And when you hear the answer, are you capable of understanding it? Or do you want the answer according to your conditioning, according to your like and dislike? That is, when you hear the answer, do you interpret it according to your particular demands and appetites? Or, are you listening *freely*? If you are listening freely and if you put the question freely, then there is a beauty in the answer. So, do you want to ask any questions?

Questioner: Is there such a thing as a soul?

Krishnamurti: S-o-u-l? Or s-o-l-e? [*Laughter*] Is there something separate from the body, from the brain, from thought, something that is timeless, that is not caught in the field of time, not time-bound? Right? That is what we generally mean by the word *soul*. Now we are going to inquire into the meaning of that word, the truth behind the word. How do you know that the soul exists at all? You have been taught, haven't you? You have been conditioned—as the communist is conditioned not to believe in a soul. You are conditioned to believe in a soul, in the Atman, in the super-ego, and so on, and the other fellow is conditioned not to believe in any of this rubbish. Now we are going to find out the truth of the matter, not your opinion and my opinion, or your experience opposed to the speaker's opinion. Is there something permanent in us? Permanent means timeless, something that cannot be touched by thought, because thought is time, thought is the past. But if you think that there is a soul, you have already brought it into time, and if thought can bring it within its field, then it is part of thought. Then the soul is not permanent; it is part of thought, and having brought about this idea of the soul as something permanent, thought takes security in that.

So the question is: Is there anything permanent which is not put together by thought, thought being experience, repetition, habit, tradition, conditioning? Is there anything that is beyond time, beyond all the measure of thought? To find that out—not as a belief or by saying 'This is so, Shankara has said this', or 'The Buddha has said that', or 'Somebody else has said that'—to really find that out, thought must be completely absent, thought being the observer. Then, if you can observe without time, you have the whole universe in your eyes, in your heart.

Questioner: After death, does the entity 'I', which tries hard to accumulate, possess, and achieve throughout its existence, and which in the process experiences alternate currents of happiness and sorrow, continue to exist through eternity, as long as it wishes to continue in the same form or in any other form?

Krishnamurti: Just listen very carefully. This question has been put by a student and it is about death, about the 'I'. It is not about what it means to *live*, to live happily, creatively, with great joy in the world. This is a typical Hindu question. In Europe and America they don't ask such a question. They ask other kinds of questions. In this country we, being so-called religious, ask these questions, which means we have divorced religion from life, from daily living. So the questioner asks: What is this 'I', and when the body dies, does the 'I' live in a different form or in the same form, and has that 'I' a continuity? Now, apparently from the question, the 'I' is considered a permanent thing, something indestructible. Is there anything in life which is not destructible? Is there anything in life which is permanent? Is your 'I' permanent? You would like it to be so, but is it permanent? Do please inquire.

What is this 'I'? Isn't it a bundle of memories? My experiences, my house, my furniture, the identification with my wife, with my children, with my furniture, with my bank account, or with a particular profession, a particular capacity? The 'me' that is angry, jealous, envious, possessive, dominating, aggressive—is that 'me' permanent? It is a memory, you understand? And is memory permanent? One would like to think the 'I' is permanent because in that, again, there is security that at least the 'I' will go on, in spite of the organism. So we cling to that. You may not call it the 'I'. You call it the Atman, the soul, the higher self, giving it different names, but it is born of the same tendency, the same drive to have something permanent in this impermanent world. And when one observes freely, one sees that there is no such thing as the 'I' as a permanent entity. Then one might ask: 'If there is nothing permanent, why cultivate any virtue? What is the point of doing anything? What is the point of all this experience?'

To find out the truth of the matter, sir, you have to go into the whole question of what is thinking, into whether thought, identified with the 'me'—my furniture, my experience, my pleasure, my fear—has any permanency. Obviously it has no permanency. What has permamency, if one can use the word, is the movement of life, not your movement and my movement, just the beauty of movement. And to move with that movement, without the observer, is to perceive something of a totally different dimension.

You know, sir, meditation is one of the most important things in life. Meditation is a marvellous thing. To understand what meditation is you have to understand the meditator. The meditator *is* the meditation and nothing else. And if you understand the meditator, you have understood the whole beginning and the end of life.

19 December 1969

The two questions I would ask if I were a student

SECOND TALK AT THE UNIVERSITY OF BOMBAY, 1969

So observe this whole phenomenon of life: getting a job, having a family, sex, pleasure, fear, pain, despair, anxiety, deepening sorrow, the enormity of all this, the complexity of all this. Just observe, not coldly as a scientist does through a microscope, but observe with tremendous passion.

If you were a student at a university, facing life and all the implications of existence, I wonder what you would ask. I should think one would ask to live a life that has deep meaning, a life not only for acquiring a house, a family, and all the rest of it, but also for finding out if there is something more than mere existence. I think these would be the two questions I would ask if I were a student: how to live in this world with intelligence, live a life in which there is great happiness, a life that one can live beautifully with great comprehension; and also how to find out if there is something more than mere superficial happiness, enjoyment, and so on. I think that is what one would ask. Can we start from there?

If you were a student just coming out of the university, facing this incredibly complex society, what would be your demand? You would want a full life, a rich life, a life that can be lived without any contradiction, freely, with great beauty and joy. Also, I am quite sure you would ask or try to find out if there is something much more profound. If we start with those questions, I wonder how we, whatever generation we belong to, young or old, would reply, what our answer would be.

One sees what life is, the everyday existence, with all the conflicts, misery, contradiction, the insistent struggle from the moment we are born till we die, the constant battle that is going on within and without, a life that is tortuous, devious, hypocritical, an existence that has very little meaning in itself but to which we try to give some intellectual explanation. Seeing all that not only in the past generation but in the generations to come and seeking something beyond the measure of thought, and not being caught in the machinery of society or culture, can one free oneself from all this entanglement and live a very simple life? If I were a student I think I would ask that: how to live a very simple life, without any conflict, how to live completely, richly, and fully, without any contradiction, so that life does not become a battlefield. Then I would ask, 'Is there something beyond all this? Is there something that man in the past has always sought?' Not to be told, not as a theory, not as speculative ideals and so on but actually. I would want to find that out actually, in the very daily living, not as an idea, not as an escape, not as something that you will get as a reward. We are going to talk about that this evening.

First, what do we mean by a simple life? The immediate answer generally given is that you must have few things, one or two meals a day. But that is only an outward show of simplicity while you are boiling inwardly, struggling, unhappy, miserable, caught in your peculiar idiosyncrasies, peculiar conditioning, yielding to your appetites, sexual or otherwise. That is the actual state:

we want to live simply outwardly, but inwardly we are tremendously complex. So where does simplicity begin? In the outer or in the inner? Can one bring about in oneself a life of great simplicity in the psychological world, in the world inside the skin? Because if there is that simplicity inwardly, obviously there will be outward simplicity. You may have one loincloth or ten loincloths. The outward simplicity then is not an exhibition to show to oneself that one lives simply.

So, what can one do to live a life in which there is *complete* freedom, without any contradiction, without going through all the battles of what should be, what has been, and what will be? Now, is that possible? Because apparently we bring about confusion and misery to whatever we touch. In our relationships there is misery, conflict, with each one out for himself and so on. Seeing all that in daily life, is it possible to live a life that is completely clear inwardly, without any distortion, without any contradiction? Because any form of contradiction means conflict, struggle. Can one live such a life? And how does it happen? Can we talk about that? Would that be of interest to you?

Look, the speaker can talk about it, but in listening to him you have to take part in it, you have to share it, and not merely sit there and exchange a few words or ideas. This isn't one man's affair: it is a mutual inquiry, a common voyage, a mutual exploration. So there is no authority. Though the speaker sits on a platform, it doesn't give him any authority. We are journeying together; therefore we are learning together, looking together, exploring together, listening to each other, so that we are moving together all the time, in step; you are not ahead of me, nor am I ahead of you. We are going to explore to find out how it happens that we can live a life in this world that is so full of complexity. As human beings, we are the result of the society, the culture, the economy, the climate, the food we eat, the tradition, the various idiosyncrasies and tendencies; we are all that. Can all that be put away so that we are really original?

To go into it, you and I must walk together, you and I must have the same passion, the same intensity. If you have no intensity, no passion to find out, you cannot take the journey. Then you are merely being inquisitive, curious, as an observer looking inside; then you have no passion to find out. To find out, whether in the scientific field or in any other field, you must have passion, intensity. If you haven't got it, how are you going to get it? Nobody is going to give it to you; there is no system, no philosophy, no method that will give you this extraordinary passion to find out. You will have it the moment you see the importance of it. The moment you are really hungry, you will find food. So, to take a journey of this kind inwardly, you must have extraordinary vitality, energy, and passion. And that comes when you see its importance. When you see the necessity, the urgency, the importance of it, you will have it.

So the question is: Why doesn't one have it first? Because without that you cannot undertake any journey, whether in the scientific or economic field or in the field of inwardness, of one's depths. You must have that. So one asks: How does one have the drive for this persistent, continuous inquiry? For that you need energy. How does it come?

I wonder what you would say if you were asked. You know, everything we do demands energy. To come here, to sit, to listen, to think; everything demands energy. Either that energy is distorted by society, by your own appetites, by your own inclinations, or it is given freedom to flow. And to let it flow fully, freely there must be no resistance, no hindrance. We are full of hindrances, resistances: 'We must do this', 'We must not do this', 'We must think this way', 'We must not think that way.' We have innumerable principles, ideals, traditions that always block us. So, can one be aware of these hindrances, these resistances, and by observing them, be free of them and not create other resistances?

Do you know what we mean by resistance? An opinion is a resistance. You have an opinion about one thing and the other has another opinion about the same thing. Each forms a resistance against the other, and so we live a life of constant resistance. Please do observe this in yourself. See what your resistances are, how you resist. And becoming conscious of that resistance, be entirely free of it so as to release energy, because the moment you block energy through resistance, it must inevitably create conflict, and to break down the resistance is to free the energy. First, one must be aware of the resistances one has, and then learn how to look so that they disappear without creating other resistances.

If you have a formula, a conclusion, that is a resistance. If you say there is God or there is no God, it is a form of resistance. You really don't know, but you have been brought up to believe. So any form of conclusion, any form of belief is a form of resistance. If you believe that you are a Hindu and I believe that I am a Muslim, obviously it is a form of division. So where there is a division there must be resistance, and that resistance invariably blocks the full flow of energy, and therefore there is conflict. That is a fact. Whether you accept it or not, that is a fact.

You have one tradition, tradition being something that has been handed over from the past, and another may have another tradition. These two traditions divide people; they are a form of resistance, and so there is division and therefore conflict. I think that is fairly clear in the sense that one can observe it in oneself.

Then what will you do, knowing that you are resisting, knowing that you have your own opinions and another has his own opinions, and you have your own conclusions and formulas as opposed to those of another? How will you dissipate them? Because if you fight against them, saying 'I must not have formulas or conclusions', then your very denial of it creates an opposite, and therefore there is a conflict.

Sirs, look. Suppose I have a belief based on my experience, my knowledge, my information, coloured by my particular tendencies, fears, and so on, and I become aware of it, conscious of it. What shall I do? Shall I battle with it? If I do, then the one who battles with it is also another form of resistance, conclusion. So, as long as I create a division between myself and my resistance, there must be conflict. So, can the mind observe the resistance, not as an observer, an outsider looking at it unrelated to himself?

As we said, as long as there is a division between the observer and the observed, and the observer says, 'I must have no resistance', he has already created another form of resistance. When he says, 'I must not', that is based on a conclusion, on a belief, on an idea. So, can the mind look without evaluation, without condemning, without wanting to change what it observes? First see the problem, then we will inquire into it.

How is one to look? The 'how' is not a method. How is one to observe without division, observe without a previous conclusion, a previous hypothesis, or a previous experience, because they act as factors of separation in observation? So I must learn to look without distortion. Is it possible at all? To look at my wife without any distortion, which means without the previous image that I have about her. I have built an image based on my experience of her—pleasure, sex, nagging, fear, domination, and so on—and through that image I observe her. Or that image observes her. Now, to be free of that image so that there is an observation without any distortion—that is the question. As long as there is an image between myself and another which creates a division, there must be resistance and therefore conflict. Becoming aware of this resistance, can the mind observe without the image? Right?

So first we must find out what is the machinery that builds images. Obviously, the machinery is experience. Please follow this closely. My wife says, 'You are stupid.' That is an experience, a challenge, and I respond. The challenge and the response bring about an experience. Now, can the mind listen to a statement by another, pleasant or unpleasant, which is an experience, listen to it at the moment so completely that it doesn't leave a mark? Can the mind listen to any statement or anybody so attentively, so completely, that the response to the challenge is totally adequate, and so there is no conflict and therefore no residue which is the machinery of building an image? That is, to live a life so that you have a thousand experiences—because they are all pouring in consciously or unconsciously—and yet have a mind that is not cluttered with images, with formulas.

Is the speaker making himself clear? Because we are taking a journey together, sharing, learning together so that it is yours, not the speaker's.

So we see how any experience builds an image, a memory. Somebody says a pleasant thing about you, flatters you, and you like that flattery. It leaves an imprint, and that imprint is going to react the next time you meet him: he is your friend. Somebody insults you and that leaves another imprint, and the next time you meet him, he has become your enemy. So when you listen to the flattery, listen to it so completely, so attentively, that it doesn't leave a mark and doesn't build an image. Can the mind do that? Can the mind do this *every time* there is a challenge, *not all the time?* You understand? The mind cannot do it all the time, it is incapable. Because that would be a tremendous strain, and it demands tremendous watchfulness. But most of our minds are inattentive, and being inattentive, when the challenge comes, we respond to it without attention. So we say to ourselves, 'I wish I could be attentive all the time.' That is, we want to transform inattention to attention; that is the desire to change *what is* into *what should be*, which is a form of resistance. So to be attentive to inattention is to be attentive. Not to say 'Inattention must be changed to attention', but to just observe the state of inattention, without wanting to change it.

So here it is. The mind, the brain, is the repository of millions of experiences—of pleasure, pain, fear, and so on—and they have built innumerable images, conclusions, opinions. Now, can one observe the totality of all that, or must they go one by one? Please understand the question before you agree or disagree. The brain has acquired through millions of years various forms of responses based on its experience. Should these responses be analysed one by one, or is there a way of dealing with them all entirely at once?

Analysis implies time. Analysis implies the analyser and the thing analysed; therefore there is a division. And when you analyse, every analysis must be complete, because if it is not complete, finished, you will apply that knowledge to the next analysis, and that may be a distortion. Also analysis, one by one, of the various responses, memories, conclusions, fears, anxieties, despairs, and hopes will take a lot of time, and you may not be capable of doing it. Even if you are capable of doing it, it involves a gradual process, involves time. And while you are occupied with the analysis of one, there are other factors coming into it. So there can be only one way of doing it: a total observation of the whole thing. That is, can the mind look at this whole structure of resistance, division, the observer and the observed, see the truth or the falseness of analysis, see all that at once?

Now just see how you respond: you say, 'It's difficult' or 'It's not possible.' When you say, 'It's difficult', 'It is not possible', or 'It is possible', you are blocking yourself. So don't agree or disagree, don't say it is possible or impossible, don't say anything, but observe. Because if it is possible you would have done it, wouldn't you? Now we are asking the impossible, aren't we? The impossible is to see the whole of the structure, non-analytically, without introducing time, without having an observer and the observed but seeing the whole thing—which is yourself—completely. And it is an *impossible* question, right? Because, your mind is accustomed to analysis, to introspection, to division, saying, 'This is right', 'This is wrong', 'This is possible', 'This is not possible', 'I wish it were different.' You are used to that. And to the mind which is used to this, a new question is being put and it says, 'I cannot do it, it's impossible' or 'It's difficult.'

Now we are asking the mind the impossible. Can the mind respond to that impossibility and respond to its possibility? You get it? You see, we never ask the impossible. We are always asking, 'What is possible? Do tell me.' The moment you ask 'how', you are asking for the possible. The 'how' means the system, the method, the practice, which is possible, but we never ask the impossible. Now you are being asked the impossible. And when you face something that is tremendous, you don't have an answer. You don't say, 'It's very difficult' or 'It's possible.' You are completely silent in front of something immense.

You know, when you see from a valley a marvellous mountain full of splendour, the very beauty of it makes you silent, doesn't it? You don't say, 'How beautiful.' You are absolutely silent in front of it. Now, what has taken place? The very majesty of the mountain has prevented you from talking. In the same way, the immense question that is being asked is making the mind silent. So then out of that silence you are going to respond; which is, whatever you do is in relation to that immensity, not to what is possible. So you have broken down all your resistances. This requires tremendous care and attention; you can't come to this just by listening to a set of words.

So one begins—not begins—one learns. One learns to look at the resistance, to look without the observer, and to let the observed unfold, tell its story. Not that the observer tells the story. The observer has no story to tell at all. The fact is telling you the story. And the fact, when it tells the story, has very little to say. But the observer has plenty to say about the fact. And that is where we get caught.

So observe this whole phenomenon of life: getting a job, having a family, sex, pleasure, fear, pain, despair, anxiety, deepening sorrow, the enormity of all this, the complexity of all this. Just observe, not coldly as a scientist does through a microscope, but observe with tremendous passion. That is, to observe with tremendous energy in which there is no conflict whatsoever. It is only such a mind that can go beyond itself.

Would you like to ask any questions? You know, we must ask questions, not just of the speaker but of everything. How you ask and how you receive the answer matter greatly. Why do you ask? Because in questioning you are opening a door. Either your door will be very small, very little, through which you look at very little things, or your question will open the door completely so that you see everything. Either your question is a small window through which you are looking and, therefore, seeing only a part of the blue sky, or you are asking a question that opens the whole of the heavens. Because in your question *is* the whole heaven, not in the reply. Because the very questioning implies that your question is based on tremendous inquiry—not for confirmation or for dialectical purposes—your very question is out of the tremendous depths of thought, of feeling. Right, sir.

Questioner: What is God?

Krishnamurti: Ah! What is God? If one were to describe it, would you understand it? Because the description is not the described. Also, why are you asking? To find out if there is or if there is not? To have a corroboration from the speaker? Or, are you asking to find out? If you are asking to find out about the immensity of life, the beauty of life, if you are asking to find out, then your mind must be free of *all* belief in God or non-belief in God; otherwise you cannot find out. If you are not free, if you are tethered to your belief, how can you find out? The atheist or the theist, the one who doesn't believe and the one who believes, both are caught; they can never find out. So before you ask if there is God or no God, there must be freedom to observe, which means freedom from all authority—no guru, no book. You must stand alone to find out. But we never stand alone. We carry with us all the books of the world. We carry with us all the gurus. The gurus don't carry you; you carry them, and they become your burden. So to find out if there is God or not, there must be freedom. That means to have no fear. And you must have a mind that is capable of looking. A petty little mind, a bourgeois mind worried about its little life and its little appetites and saying, 'This is right', 'This is wrong', 'I must have this pleasure, but not that pleasure'—how can that mind search for or ask if there is God? So, sir, before you put that question to reality—because reality can alone answer you—you must have a real mind, not a second-hand mind. You must be clear, without any distortion. Then you will never ask what God is.

Questioner: [*Inaudible*]

Krishnamurti: Oh, you would like to know about an experience that doesn't leave a mark. Is that the question, sir? Yes? Why do you hold on to your past memories, pleasant or unpleasant? Why? Why do you live in the past? If you live in the past, as all of us do, then experience is an addition to the past. So you have to find out why you always live in the past. You *are* the past. Why? Please follow this question, go into it with the speaker. Why do you live in the past, the past being your memories? In that there is great security, isn't there? Because tomorrow is uncertain. Anything might happen tomorrow. So the past becomes tremendously important because in that there is security: in tradition, in knowledge, in what other people, including Shankara, have said about life. That gives you tremendous security. And with that memory you live, and you call that living. Anything that doesn't conform to that memory you reject, and so you are in battle. You want security on the one hand, which is to live in the past—and you are the past—but life comes along and says, 'Change, break down, move', and you are frightened. So there is fear, so the tomorrow you dread.

So memory, which is the past, plays a significant, in fact the greatest part, in your life. And you say, 'How can the mind, the brain cells themselves, completely put aside all the past?' The past is the observer who says, 'I am different from you—you with your ideas, your problems, your sorrows, and I, the observer, with my problems, my sorrows.' So the observer is the past, and as long as there is the observer different from the observed, he must collect memories, and on that he lives. That is his bank account, that is his security, which is really complete insecurity. And that is why there is fear.

Questioner: [*Inaudible*]

Krishnamurti: The question is: You talk about observing the whole. How can thought observe the whole? Because there are so many other thoughts, how is one to separate one thought which will look? That is the question, isn't it? Look at the question: 'How can one thought look when there are so many thoughts going across it?' Now, do you *look at* anything with thought? Do you look at your brother or the person opposite you with thought? Do you? If you do, you are looking through the image which thought has built. Therefore to observe is to observe without thought, which doesn't mean you become neurotic and all the rest of it. You observe, knowing the whole structure and the implication and the interference of thought; knowing all that you look without it. Do it, do a very simple thing: observe a tree. Observe your brother or your father or mother, your wife or husband. Just observe without thought interfering, and you will see how extraordinarily subtle it is. Don't say 'I can't.' Then you are finished, then you block yourself. But learn how to look, learn what looking is. And when there is learning, there is no division.

22 December 1969

What is your future?

Talk at the Indian Institute of Technology, Madras, 1970

So when you look at this phenomenon around us and in us, what is the human mind to do? What are you to do? A student leaving the university, what is he to do? Not as a technocrat... But as a human being what are you going to do?

I do not know if you are aware of what is happening throughout the world. There is great discontent, revolt, and confusion, not only politically, economically, and socially, but also in oneself as a human being. We are terribly confused, and out of this confusion we are trying to find an answer that will not only be satisfactory to meet the present crisis but also enduring. One observes in Europe, in America, and in this country the deterioration that is going on. The speaker comes to this country every winter for a few months, and he has been doing this for forty-five years or so. And one sees the extraordinary explosion of population, increasing poverty, and the political mess. Also one sees here, as one does in the rest of the world, that religions have completely failed. They really have no meaning whatsoever anymore—if they ever had.

Science has not answered the human problem either, though many believed that it would resolve our confusion. And education has prepared man only for more confusion and war. So I hope you won't mind my saying that education has also failed. Because, after all, man must live in peace, so that he can think clearly, act rightly, live beautifully, and create a different world. And one must have peace in order to love. Apparently all this is not possible. We have no peace, we have no love, and all our life is a battlefield from the moment we are born till we die. The ancient traditional responses have no longer any meaning—if they ever had. So, that is the present state of the world. Religions, science, education have failed to transform man so that he can live happily with a great sense of beauty, live in a relationship which is not in conflict. But if you see all this just intellectually through one part or fragment of the mind, naturally the answer will be a fragmentary one. So the intellect, however capable—and it is extraordinarily capable—does not solve the problem, nor mere sentiment or emotionalism. Seeing this one turns to technocracy. The technocrat has now become now very important, and we say he is going to plan everything, build a new world, bring about a different relationship, and so on. But the technocrat will not answer the question either because the human mind and heart are much too complex to be understood by a segment, a fraction, of the whole of human existence.

So what is one to do? What are you and I to do as human beings, not as Hindus, Buddhists, communists, or socialists. Knowing what is actually happening in the world—linguistic, national, political, and religious divisions, and armies preparing for war—what are we to do? And communism, the thing that promised something extraordinary at one time, has now become a bureaucratic authority, a totalitarian dictatorship, though it uses words like 'proletarian government' and all the rest of that nonsense to suit its own particular theory.

So observing this strange phenomenon non-verbally, non-intellectually, and being actually faced with it, what is one to do? This is not a rhetorical question. To find this out, one has to understand certain obvious things like communication. The word dictionary meaning of the word *communication* is 'to work together, to create together'. Not that you merely listen to the one who is communicating. Communication actually means thinking, exploring, investigating together, and that is the beauty of that word. It is not the speaker on the platform communicating his ideas or theories or formulas to you who are merely listening, either agreeing or disagreeing. Unfortunately, sitting on a platform of this kind gives a certain status, a certain authority which you will kindly put aside entirely, because there is no authority here as far as the speaker is concerned. The speaker is not laying down any particular theory or doing some kind of propaganda for an ideal or a principle. What we are going to do together is to find out what to do in this world as human beings, living in an utterly confused, violent, brutal world, a world that is fragmented, where there is tyranny, where formulas and concepts are extraordinarily important, where a philosophical theory takes precedence over living. So, observing this, what is one to do, not as an individual but together? The meaning of that word *individual* is 'indivisible': not to be divided, incapable of division, separation. But we individuals are broken up, fragmented, and therefore we are not individuals at all.

So how can there be a radical mutation in the whole structure of our life? That is the real question, not more theories, more ideas and ideologies. How do we bring about a transformation, a change, a radical revolution, in the very structure of our being? That is really the question.

Religions have failed, they have not changed man; they have probably given him a little polish. Science hasn't succeeded, nor has any government, party, or philosophy. Nothing has actually changed man for millions of years. I do not know if you have seen some of the paintings in the south of France where, twenty-five or thirty-five thousand years ago, man painted pictures of his struggle against evil. And the ancient Egyptian also had the same problem of how to change man, how to change his mind. Until we do radically bring about a revolution in ourselves, we shall live in war, with violence, with brutality, and so on. We have accepted this way of life. We have accepted war, war either with the gun or war within oneself and therefore with the neighbour, with society. That is an absolute fact. So one asks oneself this question, not rhetorically, but with deep seriousness, with a deep sense of demand, because our minds—yours and the speaker's—are the result of millions of years. It is not your mind and my mind. It is the mind of human beings, who have lived for millions and millions of years, who have been conditioned, who are held in a certain particular pattern, who have lived a life of torture, misery, great sorrow. And each generation revolts against the past generation and hands to the following generation a perfect mess, of war, hatred, division, brutality, violence, despair.

And if you are a student, what is your future? Just to pass some examination, get a job, and fall into the trap which the past generation has created, get married, have a little house with a wife and children? And to fight, struggle, be thoroughly discontented, miserable? Is that what is going to happen? That will inevitably happen, though you may be a technocrat with a good salary, a car, a house, a good position, and full of your own importance.

That is what is going to happen—leading a miserable, shoddy little life. You may have a degree, do extraordinary work, help to go to the moon or to live under the sea for a month. Incredible things have been done technologically. But as human beings what are we? We lead a life which the most ancient of people have lived, with sorrow, with great confusion, with fear of death and life, without having any beauty, never looking at the beautiful sunset, or the sky, or the leaf, or the tree against the sky, concerned with our own particular little activities, self-centred, isolated in a little family, fighting, fighting. That is all we know.

We are not persuading you or doing propaganda; we are merely pointing out *what is*, and apparently it is extraordinarily difficult for most of us to observe actually *what is*. And that is what we are doing now. We are observing together exactly *what is*. Not how to transform *what is*. A good scientist observes, sees, actually *what is*, and the *what is* tells its own story. We see actually what is going on, not what is going on at the scientific or economic level but in the human mind, in the human heart, in the way we live. We are looking at it, not intellectually, not verbally, because the description is never the described, and the explanation of *what is* is not the actual seeing of *what is*. The word, the description, the explanation is not *what is*, so one must be very sensitive to and wary of words, explanations, and descriptions. And when we are clear of words then we can look, putting aside our nationalities, our petty little prejudices, and all the rest of it, and actually see what is going on.

Now, seeing *what is*, the question is: What is one to do? Will you answer it as a scientist, a technocrat, a businessman, or a scholar, or a philosopher? Answer the human problem fragmentarily? We have tried that.

This whole complex problem of living, which is the relationship between man and man, which is the society, we have tried to answer in segments, in fragments, in parts. One may be a very good scientist in the laboratory but is a shoddy little human being outside it. Even the religious man is struggling to attain what he considers reality, but surely reality can be seen only with a mind that is very clear, a mind that is innocent, has never been tortured, has never shed tears. Only such a mind can see what is truth, what is reality, that which is something beyond time, not a mind that has been caught, trapped in some philosophy, some dogma, some ideation.

So when you look at this phenomenon around us and in us, what is the human mind to do? What are you to do? A student leaving the university, what is he to do? Not as a technocrat. You will get a job, that's assured. But as a human being what are you going to do? How are you going to transform yourself so as to live a different kind of life, a life in which there is no struggle, no conflict? I don't think we realize how serious all this is, how dreadfully serious. So is it possible to bring about a radical revolution? That is the only revolution, the psychological revolution is the only revolution. Not the social, economic, or political revolution but the inward revolution, the psychological mutation, so that we can live at peace, not as an idea but actually in everyday life. To understand that, one must ask why there is so much fragmentation in the mind. You are a businessman and at home you are something else and so on. So there is contradiction when there are the opposites. Why have we divided this marvellous life with its beauty, with its extraordinary movement? Why have we broken it up? And I think in that fragmentation of the mind lies the answer, lies the answer to the challenge, the challenge being that you have lived millions of years in conflict, in sorrow, in fear, and the challenge says you must change. Because the world demands it; the present crisis demands it.

So we are together exploring why the human mind is so conditioned, broken up, fragmented in itself. If we can answer that, not intellectually or verbally, but actually in our hearts, deeply within ourselves, then we will find that we can live a totally different kind of life, at a different dimension altogether. And that is what we are going to investigate together tonight. Together—that is important to understand, because the speaker is not important at all. The speaker has no authority to tell you or ask you to do this or that. We are taking a journey together, exploring, looking, asking.

The first question is: Why is there such division, such contradiction, so much fear in the mind? (The mind, the heart, the brain, and the physical organism are a psychosomatic unit; it is not the higher self, the Atman, and the lower self and all that stuff invented by somebody.) When you are asked that question, there is nobody to answer it, no authority, no book, no guru, no professor. But you have to ask it. You have to answer this question yourself and for yourself. That is the first thing to realize: there is nobody in life who is going to tell you what to do. Others have told us what to do; the gurus, the teachers, the books, the philosophers, the analysts have all told us what to do. And so we have remained second-hand human beings for millions of years. You can repeat most beautifully, explain marvellously, intricately what others have propounded. But in essence, deeply, we are second-hand, third-hand human beings. So there is nobody to lead and for you to follow. That is one of the things you must first realize. As a human being you cannot, and must not, allow yourself to be led, either by the communist or the Marxist or by a philosopher or a psychologist or a guru. We have done all that. Because we have followed, we have made a mess in the world.

I don't think we realize how important this is. Because when you follow some authority, you become more and more dull, more and more insensitive. But if you can set aside completely all psychological, inward, authority, then you are beginning to be free to inquire. And freedom is necessary, total, absolute freedom inwardly. Freedom means not merely freedom from fear, anxiety, and sorrow, but freedom to inquire, to go deeply, profoundly into yourself, because that is all you have. You are the result of the society, the culture in which you have been brought up. That is the only thing you have, and therefore you have to investigate it, explore it, and see whether you can be completely free of all that. That is, to uncondition yourself completely. Don't say it is not possible for the human mind to uncondition itself. If you say it is possible or not possible, you have already blocked yourself, already prevented yourself from exploring. Therefore you have to ask the impossible question, the impossible question being: Can the mind be completely, wholly unconditioned? Then only can one live a totally different kind of life.

So put aside all authority inwardly, psychologically. Of course, you must have the authority of the policeman and all the rest of it because we are living in a mad, brutal world. But we are talking of deep inward freedom. That freedom is not the opposite of slavery, is not the opposite of or an escape from *what is*. So when you put aside all authority, which is quite an arduous thing to do—the authority not only of another but of your own knowledge and experience—then you can ask the question: Why can't the mind, which is such a marvellous thing and which can do the most extraordinary things, change itself? The mind is not your particular little mind, not your or my localized little mind, but the mind of man who has achieved so much. Apparently that brain, which is so capable, hasn't solved the question of living without conflict and with great intelligence, with great compassion, which means passion, not sentimentality. Why can't this brain bring about a change in itself? That is the real question. Because the brain, which is the residue of thousands of years of memories, has divided the world. That brain produces thought, thought being the response of memory, memory being experience, knowledge, the past. Why has thought not been able to resolve its own intricate, complex problem of living?

What a lovely evening it is, isn't it? Look at the new moon! You see, sirs, you never look at the new moon, you don't take time to look at it, see its beauty, its freshness, its innocence. For, you are too occupied with your own problems and your own ambitions, and you worship the terrible thing called success. That moon is there and you never see it. So you never have beauty in your life. Never! You put up marvellous buildings, create intricate machinery, but you never take time to enjoy looking at a beautiful thing. You may go to museums, but you go because you have lost touch with nature. And nature says, 'Look, look at the beauty of a tree, the loveliness of a sunset or a solitary tree in a field, the magnificence of a mountain, and the beautiful face of a woman or a man.'

So we are asking why this brain, which has had millions of years of knowledge and experience, cannot transform itself. Why doesn't it bring about within itself a total mutation? Do please ask this question, ask it with your heart, not with your petty little mind. With the fullness of your heart ask the question, and you will see, if you do ask it, that thought always replies. And the reply of thought is always old. Thought is never new, thought is never free, therefore its reply is also not new. When a question of this kind, a serious question, is put, thought pops up immediately and answers. And its answer seems to satisfy people.

Now, when the speaker asks, 'Why has the brain, which is such a marvellous instrument, not been able to solve this human agony?' it is asked as a challenge to you. A challenge must be new; otherwise it is no challenge at all. So he puts the question, and thought is going to reply. Thought always divides, divides me from you, you from another—the Hindu, the Buddhist, the Christian, the communist, and so on. Thought is very intellectual, capable, but it is the past. So the past always divides. It may be useful technologically; knowledge is necessary in the field of science, knowledge is necessary to go home, pass exams. But the past always divides, as the past, present and future. So the past is the maker of time, which is thought. And thought produces sorrow. So why can't the brain, which is such a marvellous, intricate, superb instrument, solve the human agony, misery, and chaos? Because we are always answering with thought. Do please listen to this. That is the only thing we have: thought, which is the past. And so we human beings live in the past. Every minute is the past. I do not know if you ever looked at yourself and your thoughts, the structure of your own being. If you look at it, you will see that you are the past, that you are nothing else but the past—the past going through the present and projecting the future but still the past.

So thought is time, thought is sorrow, thought is fear. Thought is always dividing, contradictory, pulling in one direction opposed to another direction or desire. So, can that brain respond anew, afresh, though it has had millions of years of experience and though it has been completely conditioned? Can that brain not respond instantly with thought? Which means, can that brain be quiet and not always jump to conclusions, not always offer opinions, judgements, evaluations, which are all based on the past? Can this brain, which is so heavily conditioned, not respond with thought? Which means, can the brain cells themselves be completely quiet when asked, when challenged?

And that is where there is meditation. That is the beauty of meditation. Not just following some method, practice, and all the rest of it, but to have the brain so extraordinarily alive and quiet that it responds intensely to any challenge. The response must be adequate to the challenge; otherwise there is contradiction. And if you respond according to the past, it must inevitably contradict, bring about a division and therefore conflict and waste of energy.

So thought divides, thought creates the observer. The observer is the past. The observer then looks and separates himself as the observer and the thing observed. There begins the whole duality, the conflict between you and your wife, your neighbour, your children, your community, and all the rest of it. And where there is conflict there is no love; you may have pleasure, sexual or other forms of pleasure, but it is not love. Is love pleasure? Is love desire? Is love pain?

Thought at one level is extraordinarily important, at the level of technology, at the level of verbal communication. It is important to think logically, objectively, non-sentimentally, not with opinions or calculated formulas. But see that thought has to be silent when facing this extraordinary human problem of living. You know, love is the only thing that is silent. You may hold a person's hand, you may smile, make a gesture, but if you look deeply, love alone is completely silent, and therefore it responds to any challenge adequately, and therefore there is no conflict. And a mind like that is a really religious mind. Such a mind needn't go to a temple or a mosque or church. Such a mind knows, is aware, observes, not as an observer observing. Truth is that extraordinary state which is timeless, measureless, absolute, whatever name you like to give to it.

Perhaps after you have looked at that moon, you could ask questions, if you care to. You know, one must ask questions not only of the speaker but about everything. But to ask the right question is very important. One can put foolish questions, and most of us do. We never put the essential question. When we do put it, we wait for an answer from somebody else. Therefore when you ask, waiting for an answer from somebody else, you are not really putting questions at all! You are interested only in getting an answer. But what is really important is to question, not to find the answer, because in the very question itself is the answer, if you know how to put the question and how to listen to it. And you cannot listen to the question if you are wanting an answer.

So if you will put a question this evening, put it not to find an answer, but to communicate together and explore into the question. And the exploration answers the question, not somebody else. This doesn't mean that the speaker is preventing you from asking questions. In questioning you are exposing yourself, and you may not want to expose yourself because you may be frightened. But one must expose oneself, as you expose your face in the mirror.

Questioner: If everybody is second-hand, who is first-hand?

Krishnamurti: A lovely question! You heard that question? 'If everybody is second-hand, who is first-hand?' Now, sir, you have asked a question; is it a serious question? To find out who is first-hand, don't be second-hand. No, please, this is not a clever answer. Don't laugh or clap. Because if that question is meant seriously, then find out whether the mind can be free of all second-hand information. That is, find out whether the mind can empty itself of the known, the past. Then you will find out for yourself what it is not to be second- or first-hand but something entirely different. But to find that out, first see how the mind is second-hand, observe it, see what its habits are, its traditions, its repetitive pleasures. Observe it, look at it, and then you will find out by looking and learning about it that the second-hand residue of others can be put aside completely. Then you are not either first- or second-hand. Then you are a human being.

Questioner: Sir, may I know what is the right answer?

Krishnamurti: Put the right question first. There is no right answer to a wrong question. But if you put the right question, there is the right answer. To ask abstractly what is the right answer, I am afraid, my lady, has no meaning.

Questioner: I meant, sir: what is the right question?

Krishnamurti: 'What is the right question?' Do listen to this. Is there a right or a wrong question or only questioning, not superficially, not out of curiosity, not out of intellectual argumentation or dialectical opinions? So there is a question or questioning only if you question with seriousness, question in order to investigate, to expose the structure of your own being. Then that is the right question. But I am afraid most of us never ask serious questions. We never want to expose ourselves to ourselves.

Questioner: [*Inaudible*]

Krishnamurti: 'What is learning?' You learn a language; you don't know Italian or French or German, and to learn to speak that language you must know many words and how to put the words together to make a sentence. That is, you learn the words, the syntax, and so on, store them up, and from there speak. That is clear and simple. Now, can you learn in the same sense about life, life which is moving, active, intense? Can you store it up, which means, having learnt you then act? That is what we do. That is, one has had an experience which has left a mark, a memory, and from that one acts. Therefore there is a contradiction, a division between the past and the action. And is that learning? So we are using the word *learning* quite differently. Learning is a movement, a constant movement. Learning about oneself is never static. Oneself is a living, moving, dynamic thing. You can't say, 'Well, I have learnt about myself, and with what I have learnt I am going to observe.' What you observe after what you have learnt is the past; the past is looking at the present. Therefore there is a division between the observer and the observed. And that is not learning. So what we have said this evening is for us to explore. In the exploration is the learning, not that having learnt, having accumulated, we act. I do not know if you have noticed that in the doing is not only the discipline of doing but also the learning. If you are a factory worker, if you go on turning the bolt over and over, year after year, you get tired of it soon, you get bored. Whereas if you are learning, you produce much more. This has been tested out.

So learning is one thing and accumulating knowledge is another. If you apply knowledge to a living thing—like yourself, a living human being with all the complexities of emotions, reactions, and responses—if you look at yourself with knowledge, you don't look at all. You are looking at it with an image, whereas if you have no image but just look, then you are learning. When you so learn there is no end. Sir, look, if you had no book, no guide, nobody whom you can possibly ever trust or have faith in, what will you do to learn, not about technological things but about yourself? Nobody can tell you what to do. You have to learn about yourself, and yourself is a living, moving thing. There is no book, no philosopher, no psychologist to tell you how to look. Therefore you have to learn. When there is learning, there is no first-hand or second-hand. When you have stopped learning, there is the second-hand and the first-hand.

Questioner: Sir, have you ever been mystically restless?

Krishnamurti: I really do not understand what that means. Physically when you are tired you may be a little restless, jittery, nervous, wiggling your foot, and also you may be restless mentally. But one doesn't understand the word *mystically*. You mean 'mysteriously'? Is that the word?

Sir, don't enter into the world of mystery. And the world of mystery is extraordinary. There is a great mystery in life. To enter into that you must be extraordinarily sane, and healthy, your mind must be very clear, undistorted.

A mind that is restless, noisy, seeking will never come upon that extraordinary mystery of life. And to come upon that is its own discipline.

Questioner: Sir, if each one searches for an answer by himself, there could be a lot of division, it could lead to different kinds of...

Krishnamurti: Quite, quite. If each one answers a question for himself, it will be contradictory and opposed to the answer given by another. Sir, when you look through a microscope, an instrument of great precision, you and the other must see the same thing. If you bring your prejudices, conclusions, hypotheses, and answers, then what you see will be something quite different from or contradictory to what is there to be seen through the microscope. What is seen through the microscope must be seen by everybody, not by you or by me or by another, as separate human beings. The seeing is important, the asking is important. And how you ask is important. If you ask the most fundamental question really seriously, not some spurious question, then the answer is not yours or the speaker's. The answer will be the truth and not dependent on anybody. When you see a danger, the danger of a pit, of a precipice, of an animal, of a snake, your reaction and another's reaction will be the same, unless one is blind or neurotic.

Questioner: What happens when the body dies?

Krishnamurti: Ah, that is a lovely question. That is an old question which the ancient Egyptians asked. I don't read books, thank God! I haven't read the Gita, the Upanishads, the Koran, or any of the philosophical, psychological, or religious books. They bore me. I would rather read a good detective story. But to answer that question: What happens to the mind, to the soul, when the body dies? You have asked this question. Do listen to it, please pay attention to it. You have asked a question. Now, who is going to answer it, and what kind of reply do you want? A reply that will be satisfactory and comforting, a rationalized answer, or an answer according to your belief that there is reincarnation? Or the answer that a communist would give, which is, it is all nonsense? So whom are you asking? This is a very serious question in itself. What happens to the mind—to the mind, not to the soul? If you say there is a soul, it means there is something permanent, something that is not touched by thought, that is not within the field of time. Because if thought touches it, it is within the field of time, within the field of memory, and therefore it is not permanent.

So, when you ask the question, 'What happens when the body dies?' first of all why do you ask it? Are you frightened of death? Death is inevitable, though the scientists may give you another fifty years. So you are frightened of dying, which means frightened of living. If you are frightened of death, you are frightened of living, because death *is* living. If you know how to live, there is no dying. Dying is not at the end of one's life, with disease, old age, decrepitude, sorrow, misery, and agony. Death means dying each day, which means living anew every day. If you don't know how to die every day, you are not living innocently every day. So you are frightened of dying because you have put it far away, round the corner, and you don't want to look at it, to let it come near you. Therefore there is fear, and out of fear you believe. And if you believe in reincarnation, which means in the next life, then this life matters enormously, not the next life. Because what you do, what you think, how you behave now matters because you are going to pay for it next life. But you don't believe in reincarnation; that is just a lovely idea. If you really give your heart to that belief, it means living now; therefore it doesn't matter what happens tomorrow.

So when there is fear of death, then that fear answers, not the meaning and the beauty of dying. Then fear wants an answer which is comforting, There is self-pity. 'I have lived so long, accumulated so much, struggled so greatly, climbed the ladder of success—is that all?' Of course, that is all because you have nothing else. You have your furniture, your degrees, you may go to the office for the next sixty years, be bullied; that is all your life is, actually, not theoretically. So being frightened of living that way, you are inevitably frightened of dying. And fear cannot answer a question of life. Therefore freedom from fear is the fullness of living.

Questioner: Sir, if there is no God, who created this monstrous world?

Krishnamurti: Sir, God has become fashionable again. Last year God was dead. I don't know if you noticed it. Quite funny, isn't it? Now, it is becoming a fashion again. God is dead in the communist world but living in this country. To find out what God is and whether or not there is such a thing, don't be an atheist or a believer. Because both are the same; those who believe and those who don't are both conditioned by their fear, their society, their culture, their environment, propaganda, and all the rest of it. But to find out that immense reality, to discover, learn, inquire, you must be free from fear and, therefore, from belief. So your inquiry whether there is a God or not is no inquiry at all. But if you ask, 'Can the mind be free of fear, the darkness that comes with fear, the anxiety, the despair that comes from fear?' then that question has an answer. And if you seriously put the question whether the mind can be free of fear, you will find that the mind can be totally, absolutely free from fear.

Questioner: You defined the past and said that one goes through the present into the future. I think you have made the present and the future vague concepts.

Krishnamurti: I said the past goes through the present to the future. And you are saying, 'The future and the present are a concept invented by thought, conceived, formulated by thought.' Is that so? Don't you live for the future? Don't you pass exams in order to get a job? And what is the past, sir? Your tradition, your memories, your experiences, the accumulated, racial knowledge. The past is the experience of the present remembered. All that is the past. And that is how we live. When we say 'I am', it is already the past.

Questioner: [*Inaudible*]

Krishnamurti: All right, sir. If you really want to know what sleep is, and whether it is necessary and what is implied in it, give attention to it. Don't just ask a question and go to sleep. Because it is a tremendous question. Sleep is necessary because the body is exhausted after a day's work. Have you noticed that darkness is necessary as light to a plant? Have you ever noticed it? If you have light all the time on a plant, it has no recuperative power. So darkness and light are necessary. So for the body sleep is necessary. But what happens during sleep? That is the question. Now, to go into that, you must journey with the speaker, not you over there and the speaker over here telling you about sleep; we must move together. What happens during the day when you are awake? You have a thousand thoughts, a thousand experiences, a thousand reactions, and many, many bruises. There is disorder in your living during the day. And as you go to bed, the mind, the brain, tries to go over what has happened during the day. Have you noticed it? Why? Because it wants to bring order. It says, 'I did this', 'I wish I hadn't done it', 'It should have been that way', and so on. It tries to bring order in the things that have brought about disorder during the day. That is why you go over what has happened. Now, when you go to sleep, the brain demands order, demands security; otherwise it can't function properly. So it tries to bring about order through dreams—frightening, ugly or very sane dreams—which are the intimations of the things that you have not understood; they are translated into dreams. So during sleep the activities of the brain go on. Because, during the day, the brain has been functioning in disorder, contradictorily, in opposition and with effort, during sleep it tries to put some order, and that order may take the form of a dream.

So if you are very orderly, not disciplined but orderly, living, watching your responses, looking at every thought, being aware during the day of your thoughts, of the trees, the animals, the road, the dirt, the squalor, the disorder in your room, the disorder in your relationship—if you watch the disorder, out of the disorder comes order, which is not a blueprint. Because you have understood disorder, out of that disorder comes order. Then, when you sleep, quite a different thing takes place. Then your sleep is complete, without a single dream. You have never asked, 'Why should I dream at all?' You have always said, 'I have dreams, they need interpretation.' But you have never asked, 'Why should I dream at all?' We say that if you dream, it is the disordered mind that dreams because you have not lived during the day with great care, with attention, watching, learning, moving. When there is order during the day, then during sleep not only do the mind and the brain refresh themselves, renew themselves, but also something else takes place, something entirely different. And that is part of meditation.

Questioner: [*Inaudible*]

Krishnamurti: Sir, would you listen? You are filled with your question, and therefore you are not listening to the answer about dreams. If you listen to that question which the speaker has gone into, you will have answered your question. Then there is no need to seek God at all. If you seek God, you will find the illusion of God. You won't find truth; you will find the illusion of truth because what you seek you project. That is what you want to find, and what you will find is what you want. Whereas to empty the mind of everything known is meditation—not the squalid thing of practice, but to find out, to inquire into the question of emptying the mind, the brain, of the past. Then you will know what truth is.

9 January 1970

The intellect will not find the answer

Talk at the Indian Institute of Technology, Madras, 1971

One sees that thought is time, that thought breeds fear and pleasure. And can thought, the everyday operation of thinking, solve the human problem? Obviously it cannot. So then what else is there that can solve this?

We seem to think that the moment we have acquired some technological knowledge at a university or an institution like this we have fulfilled all responsibility. But neglecting the vast field of life with all its complexities and merely cultivating a particular knowledge has not apparently solved any of our human problems. One may be able to go to the moon, create marvellous superstructures, live under the sea, and so on, but the problem of human relationship has not been solved. One had hoped that education would not only build a technological world where man would be freed from the machine to do other things, but also help him lead a different kind of life and bring about a different society, a different culture, a totally different religion. But education has not done that, nor has science or communism or any other kind of theoretical, ideological utopia. So we are faced with the problem of human relationship: how to bring about in relationship a tremendous, radical change. Because human relationship is society; it is the structure and nature of society. If one is at all serious—and one must be serious in a world that is so chaotic, mad, brutal, meaningless—one has to transform not only the outward structure but also the inward, psychological states of mind that make up our consciousness.

For, we are part of the world; we are not separate from the world. We *are* the world. We have created, the past generation has created this mad, stupid world. And the younger generation, if it is not careful, alert, watchful, will join the older generation in a few years and bring about another mad, stupid society. So it is a tremendous responsibility on the part of the educator as well as the student to consider what kind of world we are going to live in—not a theoretical world, not a utopia or a perfect technological world, but a world of human relationship where we can live and function in peace with each other. I think, that is a tremendous problem facing the world at the present time. One sees what is actually happening: revolt, destruction, brutality, war, anarchy. You know all that, if you are at all observant, aware of all that is going on, of the utter chaos.

And so it behoves us as human beings to see what we can do about this transformation of the human mind. Philosophies have not done it. Philosophers have spun innumerable theories, marvellous sociological or religious theories, but they have not actually changed the world. No philosophy has ever changed the world. Philosophy means the love of truth, not your truth or the speaker's truth, but of actually *what is* and also find out whether the *what is*, the actual, can be totally changed. That is what we are or should be concerned with and not talk about the theories of combustion when the house is on fire. We are confronted with a world that is aflame, chaotic, utterly confused, as human beings are. So it is the responsibility of each one of us to find out what one can as a human being do in this chaos. And there is no question whatsoever about this chaos: the political divisions, the national divisions, the regional divisions, and also the various divisions that organized religions throughout the world have brought about—the Catholic, the Protestant, the Hindu, the Muslim, the Buddhist. If you observe all this, not from a newspaper, not while sitting comfortably in a chair, observe not as a professor theorizing about it, but actually face the problem, then you are confronted with the human responsibility with regard to the problem, which is: How is the human mind, which has been put together through millennia of so-called evolution, and which is so heavily conditioned as a Hindu, a Buddhist, a communist, and so on, to bring about a radical revolution? The mind, which is the intellect, can probably bring about a physical revolution; the intellect has done that before—the communist, the French and other forms of revolution. The intellect can theorize and force people to conform to a particular pattern of society, which is what is happening in certain parts of the world.

When you observe all this, what are you, a human being living in this part of the world, to do? We cannot escape from it or withdraw inwardly. We cannot possibly escape from this chaos because we are related to it, we have bred this chaos, we have brought it into being by our daily life. So, seeing this, what can one do? Not as an individual. Because the word *individual* means 'indivisible', that is, a human being who is total, complete, not broken up. That is what the word means. As a human being he is confronted with this enormous problem, is related to that problem, not as an observer but as one taking part in it, contributing to it. So how can he bring about a transformation both outwardly and inwardly, socially and psychologically? What can he do?

I do not know if you are interested in this question at all. Most of us are not, because we have certain formulas, certain ideals and concepts through which we hope to resolve these problems. And we hope that through a particular system, whether it is the communist or any other system, we are going to change the world. Systems are created by human beings, by you, by the clever people. And we hope that through a system a particular change can be brought about. But to run the system human beings, you and I, are necessary. And because we as human beings remain as we are, when we try to run the system, we not only become slaves to the system but seek power through that system. This, again, is obviously what is happening in the world.

So what is one to do? You understand my question? You who have been educated in this place or elsewhere; you who have taken some degrees and have a job and have settled down comfortably in a little house with a wife, children, and all the rest of that; you with your particular idiosyncrasies, religious doctrines, and beliefs, stuck in a little corner, cultivating a very small part of the vast field of existence—what can you do? You know, this question is not a rhetorical one; it is put because we have to share the problem together, because it is your problem. It is your daily problem; whether you have a profession or are unemployed, whether you are a communist or what you will, it is your problem.

To discuss, to talk over together, a common problem is to find an answer, not a theoretical answer, not an ideological answer, but an actual, functional, operative answer. To discuss, to talk over together, as we are doing now, a common problem is to communicate with each other. The word *communicate* derives from the word *common*. We are sharing a problem common to all of us, understanding that problem to see if it can be solved at all. That is our responsibility. And that is what we are going to do: share, not intellectually or verbally but actually, the problem and see whether it is at all possible to bring about a change, a psychological revolution. If you bring about a physical revolution through violence, you will end up inevitably, as history has pointed out, by having a dictatorship—or the dictatorship of a bureaucracy. So physical revolution is the most primitive, meaningless revolution because in it the same pattern, perhaps modified, is repeated again and again. So what is necessary is a psychological revolution, an inward revolution. Because we are the world. The culture, the social morality—which is immoral—the social pattern in which we live, all that is created by each one of us, and to change that structure we have to change. I think, that is logical.

Then the question is, how is this possible? How is the mind, with its brain cells which have been conditioned as a Hindu, a Protestant, and so on, to undergo a radical change—not repeat the same pattern at a different level but bring about a psychological revolution in ourselves and thus bring about a totally different kind of world? Because if we cannot do that, our education has no meaning whatsoever. It may give you a job in a competitive world, but you haven't solved any problem at all. The problem is so vast that one has to apply not merely the capacity of the intellect but also all the other faculties which one has. The capacity of the intellect is to collect data as the computer does, reason objectively, and explore sanely. A good intellect doesn't come to a conclusion; it examines, explores, but if it is conditioned by personal demands, by personal prejudices, by the culture in which it lives, it is incapable of exploring, understanding. And most of us, the so-called sophisticated, educated human beings, are conditioned intellectually.

The intellect will not find the answer. That is obvious, isn't it? The intellect is efficient enough to do fantastic things like going to the moon. But the intellect divides people. If you observe, you will see how the world is divided geographically and how this division is brought about by the intellect, which is the faculty of thinking. The various forms of division—the division of nationalities, the linguistic divisions, the division between private life and public life—are all brought about by the intellect. One of the functions of the intellect, probably its major function, is to think. And throughout the world, thought, both worldly thought and religious thought, has brought about this division, and then thought tries to solve this human problem, the problem of relationship.

You see what thought has done right throughout the world. Yet thought tries to solve this human problem which it has brought about. So you have to understand the whole structure and nature of thinking, not according to any philosopher or psychologist but by actually observing your own thinking. Perhaps what I am going to say may sound heretical. Because you have read so many books, you are full of knowledge—of what other people have said, of the Gita, the Upanishads, and all the rest of it. But you don't know what you think, what your own original thinking is—if you have any. Because you are second-hand human beings, piled up with other people's knowledge, you don't know a thing for yourselves.

So here is a problem which both of us have to share to find the truth of the matter. One sees what is actually happening in the world: the division, the conflict, the contradiction, the political corruption; you know all that is happening, we don't have to go into all that. Thought has brought this about, thought which is the response of memory, experience, knowledge, which is the past. Thought is the response of memory, the memory that you, your race, or your ancestors have accumulated through millennia. It is stored there consciously or unconsciously, and that storehouse is the brain. If you observe yourself, the way you talk, the words you use, your behaviour, then you will see that your mind—which is also the brain cells—is the repository of all experiences, not only your personal, immediate experiences, but all the past, racial experiences. Those brain cells hold all the memory, hidden and open. And any response from that memory is thinking. If you had no memory, you wouldn't be able to think at all. (Perhaps that may be fortunate.) So thought is the response of the past, which is knowledge, and so thought can never be free; thought is always old. This again is an absolute fact.

And we try to solve all our human problems through the only instrument we think we have, which is the intellect, which is thought. We also see that thought has divided people. And thought, not being able to solve this human problem, has constructed a super-ego or the super-Atman, which it hopes will solve our problems. But that idea of the super-self is part of thinking. Thought is time, the result of time, and so the super-Atman, the Brahman, the soul, or whatever you like to call it, is part of time and therefore not real. It is real only in the sense that thought has constructed it. So this world, the society, the culture, the human relationships, the divisions have all been brought about by thought, by your thinking. I think this is obvious; it is not just a conclusion. When one observes, explores deeply this problem, one can see that thought has brought about this division, conflict, and misery.

So thought as the intellect, however capable of reasoning, cannot possibly solve this problem. Your thinking, however subtle or shallow, is the result of the past. The past has been put together, and what has been put together, horizontally or vertically, is time. Anything that has been put together demands time; the brain cells, all the collection of memories, are the result of time. And we hope that time, which is thinking, will solve our human problems. But one can see that they can *never* be solved through thought. Right? One sees that thought is time, that thought breeds fear and pleasure. And can thought, the everyday operation of thinking, solve the human problem? Obviously it cannot. So then what else is there that can solve this?

To answer that question, one has to go into this problem of perception, seeing. A mind is incapable of seeing clearly when it has any form of conclusion or prejudice. When you look at the world as a Hindu or a Muslim, when you look through a particular little hole called Hinduism, communism, or what you will, how can you see the totality of anything? So one has to be free of this conditioning to understand the complex human relationship.

One has to understand also the principle of pleasure because most of our morality and activity, our search and striving are based on the principle of pleasure, aren't they? Observe it, you can see it for yourself. Our ambitions, the desire for success, the competitive pursuit, the aggression, the violence, the relationship between people are based on the principle of pleasure. And without understanding pleasure and fear we shall never know what love is. So we must understand what pleasure is, what fear is, what love is, and understand also the immense problem of death and whether there is a reality not invented by thought. To understand all that we must be able to perceive, look, not through the eyes of another, look at not what the analysts, the psychologists, the professors, or the philosophers say, but look with our own eyes. We have to examine what pleasure is, and that is a very important question because, in the understanding of that, you will understand what love is. You will also understand then if there is or there is not something beyond the things that thought has put together. So let us briefly inquire together into what pleasure is. Is pleasure love? Is pleasure desire?

Please, you are not just listening to the speaker, but actually observing yourself, your own pleasures, your own demands, your own pursuits. Watch them and find out. Though the speaker is going to describe, realize that the description is never the described. So what is pleasure, which every human being pursues most subtly or most crudely, sexually, and in so many ways? What is that thing which man pursues endlessly? When you see a lovely sunset, when the whole sky is filled with a roseate glow, as it is now in the west with the setting sun, you experience a great delight. That is an experience. That experience gives you great delight, and you pass on to other things. But the mind, the brain cells, have registered that delight, and there is the demand for the repetition of that. Please watch it in yourself: you want the repetition of the delight you had when you saw the sunset. That is, the memory of that sunset has been registered, and the thinking about that incident, that experience, that happening, gives it continuity as pleasure. You have had a sexual experience or other kinds of experiences. You think about it, you chew over it—image after image—which is, thought thinking about a past event sustains and gives continuity to pleasure.

So thought creates and gives continuity, nourishment to both pleasure and fear. That is, you have had a pain, a physical discomfort, suffering, both physical and psychological. This happened several days ago, last wee or last month, and you think about it hoping that it will not happen again. So thinking about something which you don't want to happen but may happen is the beginning of fear. So thought sustains pleasure and fear.

But joy, ecstasy, or an immense sense of delight has nothing whatsoever to do with thought. It happens. It happens when you are not occupied, when your mind is not chattering. You suddenly find a great sense of delight, beauty and joy. Then thought comes along and says, 'I would like that joy to be repeated.' Then that joy, which was so natural, unexpected, becomes pleasure. So thought is the response of the past memory; which means thought is the response of knowledge. There is the response, the challenge of death. And you respond according to the memory of the known. The known is of yesterday: what you know, your experiences, the images of your family, the knowledge that you have accumulated, all that you have collected. That is the past, and of that the mind, the brain, is a slave. Therefore it is frightened of what may happen tomorrow, of the unknown, of death.

One sees how thought has divided the world geographically for economic reasons, divided people linguistically, nationally, and racially, and also how thought everlastingly pursues pleasure and always avoids fear. Fear is the result of thinking about what might happen—that you might lose your job—and therefore being afraid there is violence. All this is the result of both rational intelligence and irrational intelligence. The intellect, which is rational, capable, and efficient and also irrational, neurotic, conditioned, and illogical, has created not only the social structure with all its morality, its economic divisions and injustice, but also this everlasting conflict, battle, in us. So see all this, not abstractly, not verbally, because if you see it verbally, through a newspaper, through a book, through what other people say, then you will live a mechanical life; then you will not be directly in relationship with life. Seeing this and realizing what thought has done, what is one to do? You understand the problem? What are you? You are educated—whatever that word may mean—which is merely cultivating a little corner of the vast field of existence. And from that little corner you think you are going to solve all problems, and therefore you disregard totally the rest of the field. I do not know if you have observed this in yourself. If you have not, do please observe it now. If you live in and function from a little corner hoping to understand the whole field, you must obviously live a life of contradiction, a life of effort, torture, misery.

So one has to look at life with eyes that are not conditioned. And there is the problem whether the mind with its brain cells can free itself completely from the past and look anew. Knowledge is necessary. Otherwise you can't go from here to there, you can't function, you can't be a good technician, you won't be able to talk English or Tamil, you won't be able to recognize your wife or your friends. So knowledge is essential, but it becomes a complete hindrance when thought, functioning from the past which is knowledge, operates. You cannot put aside knowledge and become a primitive, go back to tribalism. Knowledge is necessary, but yet you see that knowledge in human relationship creates conflict.

Look, sir, it is very simple. If you are married or if you have a friend with whom you have lived for a number of years or a few days or a few weeks, you would have built an image of each other. You would have put together an image about her or him. That image has been put together through various insults, nagging, dominance, disregard —you know what relationship is, especially between a husband and wife. That image is the past, and the relationship between those two images you call relationship. You leading your own private life and she leading her own private life, you with your ambitions and she with hers—these prevent actual relationship. I don't know if you see this at all. That is, the past, which is time, destroys all relationship. Now, the question is: Knowing that thought has its limited function, how can there be a radical psychological change which is not touched by thought? You have understood my question? Thought obviously cannot change the pattern which it has built or will build, because thought is the past. So, is there a movement, a psychological movement, which is not of the past?

You see, sir, to find out if there is God or no God—not whether you believe in God or don't believe—you have to put aside all belief, put aside totally every form of fear, every form of conflict. You have to totally understand what pleasure is because, if you don't, you have no basis for order. Order is virtue, not something you cultivate, not something you practise. Order comes into being only when there is an understanding of disorder, the actual disorder in which you live: the hypocrisy, the conflict, the agony, the despair, the confusion. When you begin to understand that disorder, not correcting it, not saying, 'It must not be' or 'must be', but actually observing it in your daily life, then out of that comes order which is living. If you have this absolute order, which is righteousness, which is action in which there is this sense of non-division, then you have the foundation for meditation. And then there is the possibility of finding out whether there is or there is not something beyond time.

I wonder if you would like to ask questions.

Questioner: [*Inaudible*]

Krishnamurti: Wait, wait. You see, sir, that gentleman hasn't listened to a word of what has been said. He is full of his own questions, and when you are full of your own questions, you don't want to hear an answer because you have your own answer already. So if you are going to ask a question, ask it not to find an answer from the speaker; ask it so that you find the answer for yourself. Because in the asking you will discover how serious you are, whether you are expecting an answer according to Marx or Mao, or some Indian philosopher or saint. By asking questions you are going to find out, and by asking and listening to what the speaker has to say, you become capable of exploring for yourself. Therefore you don't depend on anybody; you are free to find out. Then you don't need a guru; then you are your own teacher and your own disciple. Therefore one must ask questions, one must doubt. But doubt is a dangerous thing. It must always be kept on a leash; otherwise you keep on doubting, and that has no meaning. And to ask a question, you must listen not only to what the speaker has to say but also to the other questions that are going to be put. Which means you must have the capacity to listen totally, not intellectually or in abstraction but actually, with your ears, with your hearts, with your minds. Then you learn, but you stop learning if you are merely theorizing, wanting confirmation of your own petty little conclusions or beliefs. And if you listen totally to your questions and so to the questions of the others and also to the answers, you will ask no further questions at all because you will have a mind and heart that can learn. All this is said not to prevent you from asking questions. On the contrary, it is to point out the beauty of questioning and the beauty of listening to the answer which you may find for yourself or from another.

Questioner: [*Inaudible*]

Krishnamurti: 'Is it possible to observe the psychological movement without thought, without the movement of thought?' Is that right, sir?

Look, I want to know myself, I want to know what I am, not according to any religion, any teacher, any philosopher, any analyst, or psychologist. I want to know myself as I am, not as I should be. So I have to look at myself, look at myself as I am, without any interpretation, without saying, 'It is good', 'It is bad', 'It is ugly', 'I must change', 'I must not change.' You can't change the sunset, you can't do anything about it. You just look. In the same way you have to just watch, observe yourself.

Now, is that observation a movement of thought? That is, can thought look at the movement which it has created, which is the 'me'? The 'me' is a bundle of memories, conditioned, put together through time, through experience, through knowledge. That 'me' is the result of time, of thought; whether that 'me' is the super-me or the super-Atman, it is still part of thought. All that is the 'me', the 'I', the ego, the self-centred activity. Now, can that which thought has created be observed by thought, by the movement of thought?

Look, sir, put it differently: I am all this bundle collected through centuries upon centuries, through the environment, through the race, through knowledge, through time. That 'me' is the observer, the censor who says, 'This is right', 'This is wrong', 'This should be done', 'This should not be done.' The observer looks, and what he looks at is the psychological movement of which he is a part. Let us put it a little more simply. You are envious. You know what it means to be envious: comparing yourself with somebody who has got more, or less. Now, there is that response which is verbalized, named as envy. At the moment of that response, when you are envious, there is no observer at all; there is only a state of envy. A few seconds later the observer, which is the thinker, comes along and says 'I should not be envious', or gives explanations or reasons for why he should not be envious. So he separates himself from envy, he becomes the censor, the observer, and then controls or suppresses or goes beyond the envy. So there is the observer and the observed, and in that there is division. That division is the source of all conflict, not only outwardly but also inwardly.

Now, can you observe, or is there an observation, without the observer? There is the palm tree. Can you look at it without the observer, the observer who names it a palm tree, who looks with like and dislike. You may be able to look at the palm tree objectively because it doesn't affect you. But can you look at your wife or your husband or the man who insulted you, without the censor, observe without the past records? If you can so observe, then that observation is not the movement of thought.

Questioner: You say that modern society is corrupt and also that a confused mind does not work clearly. How do you feel that modern society can lead to a revolution?

Krishnamurti: The questioner says that modern society is corrupt and that a mind confused by conclusions, by various forms of conditioning cannot possibly bring about a real revolution, inwardly or outwardly. And he goes on to ask: How can such a mind, which is so bound by conclusions, formulas, and slogans, bring about a revolution? Is that the question, sir? Also, when I say that modern society is corrupt, the questioner says, my own mind has come to a conclusion and therefore it judges.

Questioner: You have no right to have such an opinion...

Krishnamurti: 'You have no right to have such an opinion.' Sir, I don't think it is an opinion or a conclusion, I don't think it is something that I have put together in my own mind. You can observe this. You observe how man is confused, you can observe the division in the world, the division between the communist and the capitalist, the Catholic and the Protestant, the Hindu and the Muslim. This division does breed conflict, and to say that division brings about conflict is not a conclusion. It is a fact, as factual as this microphone is here. You have had wars between Muslims and Hindus; that's a fact. Division breeds antagonism, resistance, conflict. And when you observe this, you say division brings about conflict. That is not a conclusion. You are merely stating a fact.

Questioner: Why do you talk at all?

Krishnamurti: Oh, why do I talk at all? I really don't know. [*Laughter*] Do you ask a flower, 'Why do you flower'?

Don't clap, sirs, do listen to this. This is not being clever. When you see something beautiful, do you ask, 'Why are you beautiful'? One generally talks with a motive: to convert somebody, or by addressing a large audience like this, to feel terribly important, or derive a great deal of encouragement and energy, as the politicians do. If there is a motive for talking, then it is exploitation. I have no motive in talking. If you want to listen, listen; if you don't, don't. You neither encourage the speaker nor discourage him. Take it or leave it. It is your life, your misery, your sorrow that we are concerned with. And if you don't want to end your sorrow, your confusion, the agony and the torture of your life, don't listen. Nobody is asking you, forcing you, to listen. This is not propaganda. Propaganda always means telling lies. We are concerned with changing *what is.* And just as you don't ask a flower why it blooms, don't ask the speaker why he speaks.

Questioner: [*Inaudible*]

Krishnamurti: 'Would you please talk about or explain why there is so much difficulty in communication between individuals?'

As we said earlier, we are not individuals at all. We think we are individuals, but that is merely a word which has very little meaning. When you look up that word in the dictionary, you find that it derives from the Latin word *indivisible,* which means 'not capable of being divided, broken up'. How can two human beings who are broken up in themselves communicate with each other, communication being sharing, cooperating, working, creating together? There is the possibility of communication when two human beings have a common problem and are deeply concerned with the solution or the understanding of that problem. When you are deeply concerned you can commune both verbally and non-verbally, but if one human being has certain opinions, conclusions, ideas, and the other has opposing ideas, how can there be communication between the two? If you are a Hindu and I am a Muslim, how can we communicate? There is a possibility of communion only when both you and I are free of our petty little ambitions. That means, when we are really individuals—indivisible—then communion between us is possible. That means, when there is love between us, not opinions or conclusions, when we really care dispassionately, intensely, there is the possibility of communion.

Questioner: [*Inaudible*]

Krishnamurti: 'How do you bring about order when there is so much disorder?'

Questioner: And bring about an attitude that is indivisible.

Krishnamurti: First of all, do we know we live a disorderly life? Don't you know that you lead a disorderly life—a public life and a private life, wanting this and wanting that, having ideals and living a life without any relation to the ideals? You have the ideal of non-violence, haven't you? But you actually live a violent life. So this contradiction, this dual existence, which brings about conflict, is disorder. Are you aware of your life as disorder? Look at your own life and find out. You think one thing, say another, and do something else. This hypocritical existence—having an ideal and living entirely different from that ideal—is disorder, isn't it? You see how silent you are. And you ask how order can come out of this terrible disorder. Now, just listen. Don't agree, but listen to find out for yourself the truth or the falseness of what is being said.

If you become aware of the disorder of your life, not only outwardly but inwardly too, you ask what has brought about this disorder. When you ask you are looking for a cause, aren't you? And to analyse and find out what the cause is takes time, doesn't it? You can easily find out why—the culture, the society, the family, the tradition, the racial inheritance; those are the causes. Now, to examine all the causes which have brought about this disorder requires time, requires days. And while you are examining, taking time to find out the cause, your life is still in disorder. So it is a waste of time, waste of energy to find out what has brought this about. What you can do is to observe that disorder, observe without trying to bring about order, without saying to yourself, 'I must bring order' or 'I trying to suppress this disorder.' Just observe it as you observe that sunset. You can't do anything about that sunset. In the same way, observe that disorder without any choice, be aware of that disorder, and you will see that, if you are really aware, out of that awareness comes an order which is an extraordinarily living thing. That order is not according to any blueprint, it is not a mechanical order. Therefore look at disorder, listen to it, observe it in yourself. And the observer *is* the cause of disorder, the observer is part of the disorder. Therefore you must look without the observer, and then you will see what comes out of it.

17 January 1971

Why are you being educated?

Talk at the Indian Institute of Technology, Bombay, 1984

So, if one may ask, are you wasting your life—life which is so complex, life which has no readymade answers? Life is vast and therefore is something most extraordinarily sacred. And what do we do with it?

One wonders why in a place like this you are being educated. For what? What is the relationship between this institution and the world? What relationship has knowledge—of science, biology, and so on—to the world? Throughout the world students are all being educated in various disciplines, and so one must ask where, after all these years of elaborate study and acquisition of a great deal of knowledge, it is all ending up. What place have your scientific and other disciplines actually in this world? The existing world is the world in which we live our daily life. Whether we live in America, Russia, Europe, India, or Japan, that very life is being threatened by war, not only conventional war but also nuclear war. Top scientists have written about what they think will happen if there is a nuclear war. They say that the whole earth will be covered by a thick layer of dust and smoke and so sound will not be able to penetrate that, and the temperature will fall to four or five degrees below zero. So, at the end of a nuclear war, not a living thing will exist on the earth. So there is this activity of human beings: highly technological, with each technician being concerned with his own particular life, with his own particular discipline, and totally disregarding what is happening to human beings throughout the world.

Also, one observes that this technological advancement is so vast, so tremendous and rapid and it may lead to extraordinary results. Added to that is the computer, which probably will take over most of the activities of human beings. It may perhaps not be able to write, compose music like Beethoven, Mozart, or Bach, but it will do most of the things that human beings are now doing. Then what is going to happen to the human brain?

So there is the technological world and the human world. We have given tremendous importance to the technological world, and that is why you have this institution with its various disciplines. And we seem to neglect, perhaps totally, our whole way of living, what is happening to man, what is happening to you as a student or as a professor. What is your relationship to the world, to all the horrible things that are happening? They are inventing the instruments of war that can destroy the whole of humanity with one blow. This is not an exaggeration by the speaker, this is a fact. In America they have been talking a great deal about what will happen if there is a nuclear war. Ten million people in New York will evaporate, as also a thousand million people within a radius of hundred miles. Technology is developing on that side. Then there are the horrors that you see in this country, especially in towns like this where human beings live in hovels, live in dirt, squalor, and misery and breed children. Human beings have, during the last forty-five thousand years, acquired every kind of knowledge. And we end up like this—with war, destruction, hatred, misery, utter confusion, and sorrow.

On the other side, man is trying to find something beyond himself, beyond his own misery, his own selfishness, his utter insufficiency, and lack of affection. And he invents gods; in this country, I believe, there are over three hundred thousand gods, and vast sums of money are spent on all that. We were told the other day that a temple in south India earns a million rupees every third day. So we are asking you, professors with their knowledge and students acquiring knowledge and searching for a vocation: What has all that got to do with your daily living? Or, are you so enclosed in your own institution, enclave, that you forget the world? So we are asking: What place has all your knowledge—we are not against knowledge—in your relationship to the rest of humanity?

We are inquiring together into what place has knowledge in the world of human relationship, what place has all the scientific information that you have gathered, stored in the brain as memory. Knowledge is never complete, whether in the future or in the past. Knowledge is never complete because the experience from which knowledge arises is limited, incomplete; there can be no complete experience. From experience, knowledge gets stored in the brain as memory, and from that memory arises thought. And thought is the very essence of knowledge. The thinker is knowledge, the activity of knowledge, and the thought of the thinker is also part of knowledge. There is no thinker apart from thought. And thought has created all the things of the world—great painting, poetry, music, and so on. Thought has created everything except nature. The tiger has not been created by thought, nor that lake which you see every day. (Probably you have got used to it, and so you hardly ever look at it.) Man has not created the heavens and all the things on the earth. Thought has no relationship to all that. But thought has invented gods. Thought has produced the most marvellous architecture, the great temples of this country, the great mosques, the great cathedrals of Europe, and all the things that are in them.

And thought is limited. There is no complete thought; thought can never be complete. It can imagine that it can measure the heavens, but it is always limited. And the technological world is also the product of thought. Without thought you could not produce a submarine, go to the moon, or invent the nuclear bomb. Thought has been responsible for all this.

So, what is your response to all this, not to just one particular aspect of life but to the whole existence of man, that is, your whole existence from now till you die? What is the meaning of all this? What is your answer, your response to the world and to your vocation, which is mere imitation, conformity? What is your relationship with your neighbour, with your wife or husband? And what is your relationship to the rest of humanity? If you have at all thought about these things, you must have an answer. As the biologists and others point out, we have lived on this earth for forty to fifty thousand years. We have gone through wars, insecurity, misery, great anxiety, confusion, uncertainty. After all these thousands and thousands of years we are still very primitive. We may be advanced technologically, but inwardly, in the psychological world, which always dominates the outer, we are still primitive, brutal, violent, selfish, superstitious, and frightened. We keep the two—the external world and the inward life of daily travail—completely separate. You may be great technicians, have excellent theories about human nature, but all that is the movement of memory and knowledge and has nothing whatsoever to do with your daily behaviour. The two are divorced—the word and the deed—and that is what we are being educated for. So our education, our knowledge will always be limited. And what has knowledge to do with human relationship? Doesn't knowledge kill love?

May I go on with what I am saying? This is not a lecture to inform or instruct you. If I may most respectfully point out, you are not merely listening to the speaker's words, intellectually grasping certain concepts and ideas. We are having a dialogue, a conversation, about the whole of existence. So, please, you are taking part in what the speaker is saying, not merely listening to certain words. We live by words, our whole brain is a network of words, but words are not the actual. But we are so caught up, so conditioned by words, by language, by tradition, by knowledge that our brains are never free.

We are problem-solving machines, aren't we? We have been trained from childhood to learn mathematics, history, physics, and so on. All that becomes a problem at school, in college, and university. So we become problem-solving machines and thus make life into a vast, dreadful problem. There is great misery, poverty, brutality in this country. When you drive down Bombay you see all those filthy huts, tents, where human beings live. You want to cry when you see all that, and nobody cares. You listen to all this, but it makes very little dent on you. Governments don't care, individuals don't care, because they are concerned only with themselves, with their knowledge, with their power, with their money. And students throughout the world are being trained to seek a vocation of imitation—pass examinations, get a degree, a Ph.D, and get a job either in this country or in America. As I was informed this afternoon, thirty per cent of you probably go to America, where you make a lot of money. That is where all your knowledge is leading you to. So we are asking: If you are at all serious, what is your response to all this? Either you withdraw from it all, join some cranky institution or *ashram* or some gurus who make tons of money. Or you enter into the world and get caught in it. Or you live a life of your own.

So what is the purpose of your existence, what is the meaning of your existence? Please, the speaker is asking this in all humility. Is life's purpose merely to earn money, to be married, have a house, power, position? Is that the purpose of your life? Apparently it is. That is what you are all being trained for, that is what you want. And if you are dissatisfied with that, then you invent a purpose—to find God or some kind of illumination. If that too doesn't satisfy you, you take to drugs and drink and all the rest of the vast amusement. One wonders if you realize what the entertainment industry is doing to you. Then there is the religious entertainment of going to temples, doing puja, and all the circus that goes on in a temple or a church or a mosque. Please don't get annoyed, I am just pointing this out. What is the purpose of all this? We have lived on this earth for forty to fifty thousand years, we have evolved, we have gone through great many tears, laughter, pain, anxiety, and yet we remain what we are—selfish, narrow-minded, concerned with ourselves. That is an actual fact.

So, if one may ask, are you wasting your life—life which is so complex, life which has no readymade answers? Life is vast and is therefore something most extraordinarily sacred. And what do we do with it? You have to answer this question, whether you are old or young.

So, as students and professors, what is your response, your responsibility? You see, you have always had leaders, especially in this country. You have had great leaders, political, social, religious, and so on. And where have they led you? Where has Marx led the communist world? Where have all the so-called sacred literature, the Upanishads, the Gita, led you? There is nothing sacred about them, no book is sacred. So what is the meaning of all this existence? You may not want to look at it, you may want to avoid it. You may say, 'I am too young, it is not my business.' And the older people say, 'Sorry, we are too old, we cannot face all this anymore.' So what is all your knowledge leading you to? To conformity, imitation? To mere absorption of information so that there is nothing original, nothing pristine?

What place has knowledge in love? Is not knowledge the enemy of love, the destroyer of love? Would you please consider this? You give about twenty or thirty years to acquiring knowledge of physics, linguistics, biology, sociology, philosophy, psychoanalysis, psychiatry, and so on. You give years and years to it, and you don't give one day or even one hour to find out for yourself what you are and why you are living like this.

And have you realized that all human beings, whether they live in affluent societies, in castles or in huts, share this human consciousness. Because all human beings suffer, go through great agonies, a great sense of loneliness, despair, and the meaninglessness of this existence. All human beings on this earth—which is so extraordinarily beautiful and which you are so sedulously destroying—whether they are the poorest and the most illiterate or the highly sophisticated, suffer, go through a great sense of desperate loneliness, and face death. Every human being on this earth shares all this. Do please listen to what the speaker is saying, don't get bored. Nobody is going to tell you all this. We share the common sorrow, the sorrow of the whole of mankind. Our consciousness is made up of all this. Your consciousness is not yours, though your tradition, both religious and social, says you are a separate individual. Your consciousness is what you are: your beliefs, your superstitions, your fears, your anxieties, your lack of love, and your selfishness. It is the consciousness of all humanity. There is no escape from that; it is a fact. Therefore you are not an individual. You may be a woman or a man, you may be tall, have fair skin, and so on, but you are not an individual. You are the whole of humanity because you smile, you laugh, you shed tears, you go through great turmoil, effort, and conflict, and face insecurity. So you are actually the rest of mankind. You are not a Hindu, though you like to call yourself one. That is just your local, provincial conditioning.

So facing all this, are you going to waste your life—passing some examinations, getting a job, being trained to imitate? That is what you are being taught—to imitate, to conform, to fit into the pattern. And is that the end of life? Then you will ask, 'What shall we do? Is there something else?' To find something totally different from all this, you have to have a great deal of intelligence. Intelligence is not knowledge. Knowledge gives you capacity, position, status, but knowledge is not love, knowledge is not compassion. It is only where there is love and compassion that there is intelligence, and that intelligence has nothing whatsoever to do with the cunning intelligence of thought.

So, if the speaker may most politely ask: Are you wasting your life? This is the only life you have. You may think there is reincarnation, that you will be born next life. That may be a mere theory. Even if you believe in reincarnation, what matters is how you live now, whether you are good, whether you are a total human being, not broken up as a scientist, biologist, as someone with a special career. If your life is broken up, if there is conflict, your life is never a holistic movement. So considering all this, ask yourself if you are wasting your life. Nobody can answer that question except yourself. The speaker won't tell you, because it is absurd, unintelligent, stupid, to say what the purpose of life is. The purpose of life is what you are doing now: study, or if you have already a job, earn more money, have more status, more power. That is what you want, and that is the purpose of your life.

Also, we have to face the ultimate thing, which is death. You may not, as you are all young people, but it is there for you as well as for the older generation. You see, it is always there. And can you live with death? That requires a great deal of inquiry: to live with death. Not commit suicide, not run away from death, but to know the depth and the greatness and the tremendous vitality of death. This is the whole of life—to be able to inquire into the whole psychological world, to understand all that. Not from books, not from philosophers, not from your professors, but to learn from yourself what you are. And you will discover, if you go into yourself, that your whole life is based on becoming something—the clerk becoming the manager, the reader becoming the professor, the chief minister becoming the prime minister, and so on. You are always trying to become something outwardly and inwardly. This is what we call living—never a moment of quietness, never a moment of great beauty in our life, but only the incessant chattering of the brain. Don't disregard all this because the psychological world, the inner world, what you are inwardly, overcomes whatever the social structures or the governments establish. You see it in Russia: they started out by having no government, no army, no division, no nationality; they said governments would disappear. But the psyche was far stronger than the superficial social structure, and so they have now the privileged, the top people who have everything in the world, the best of everything, like the top people here.

So what are you going to do after listening to this talk? Is your brain open to all this? What is your responsibility? Is it a global concern or your own narrow little yard, the narrow little self, the 'me', which is a very small affair? Are you going to be concerned with the whole world? Which means you cannot be an Indian anymore, you cannot be a Christian, a Hindu, a Buddhist. All those divisions are destructive, they have no meaning. We have to build a new civilization, a new culture, a new way of looking at life.

Do you want to ask any questions?

Question: Knowledge of any kind cannot be bad. What could possibly be bad is the use it is put to. In my opinion, the call of the day is to acquire or cultivate knowledge of using knowledge properly for proper causes. Kindly comment.

Krishnamurti: Who is the user? Who is the entity that is using knowledge properly or wrongly? Is not the entity, the user of knowledge, himself knowledge? You say that if we use knowledge rightly it's all right, but it is the wrong use of knowledge that's wrong—that is bluntly put. But the speaker is asking the questioner, 'Who is the user who uses knowledge rightly?' Is not the user, the thinker, also knowledge? Is he separate from knowledge? Or is the problem not the right or wrong use of knowledge, but what place it has? Knowledge has its right place, which is to drive a car, to write a letter, or if you are carpenter, to use the knowledge that you have acquired about the shape of the wood, the quality and grain of the wood, and so on. There you need knowledge.

But does one need knowledge about oneself? Because oneself *is* knowledge. I don't know if you understand this. If I may most respectfully point out, your question is wrong; you assume that the user of knowledge is different from knowledge. Who are you who is going to use knowledge? Are you not the result of centuries of knowledge, conscious and unconscious? 'You', the self, is knowledge. But you are dividing knowledge from the entity that uses knowledge, but both are based on knowledge. So we are saying that knowledge has a definite place in the world of daily activity. But psychological knowledge, that is, the knowledge you have about your wife or husband is divisive, it prevents love. You can see this simply. You have an image about your wife, and the wife has an image about you, and the images are built through knowledge. You have lived with her twenty years or five days, and you already have got knowledge of her. So you have built an image about her. And the images have relationship, not you and the woman or the man. These are all facts, if you examine them closely.

Question: As you said, we are problem-solving machines, which means machines meant for research and scientific investigation. Do you think, then, that all the problems of humanity would be solved if life is organized from the point of view of developing, producing, and maintaining the machine scientifically in order to promote research and science and not left to develop haphazardly as is happening today?

Krishnamurti: May I tell you a story? Two friends are walking along a street, and one of them picks up something from the pavement, and as he looks at it his face becomes tremendously illuminated, happy, he cannot hold himself. And he keeps looking at the extraordinary thing he has picked up. And his friend asks, What did you pick up? You look so happy, radiant, something has happened to you.' The first one says 'I have picked up truth.' And the friend replies, 'Marvellous, let's go and organize it.'

You see the point of the story? You want everything organized, put in their categories. Organization demands hierarchy, and we are used to hierarchies, political, social, and religious, somebody always in authority above you. And what does authority do to you? Of course, the professor knows more about physics than you do, the surgeon knows than the beginner in medicine. But why do you need hierarchy, authority in the spiritual world? Forgive me if I use the word *spiritual*, because that word has been misused. Why do you want an authority on yourself? Who is going to tell you about yourself? Your professor? Volumes have been written from the ancient of times about what you are, and probably some of you have read them, but you remain what you are. And you want what you are to be organized? Organization in certain areas is necessary, but in the psychological world it is destructive. Because then we psychologically become slaves to organizations.

Question: Throughout your talk you claimed that there is a lot of confusion in this world. But I do not remember your having given a suggestion or a solution regarding that. Don't you think that this adds to the confusion rather than reduce it?

Krishnamurti: Certainly. Certainly it produces more confusion. But confusion is there; I don't claim it. Walk down any street in Bombay or Paris or New York, and you see a great deal of confusion. That is a fact. It would be absurd if I claimed it, for it is a fact. The fact is that where there is confusion there is conflict, like between the Arab and the Jew. They are fighting each other, killing each other, and that is the essence of confusion. It is not that *I* claim it; it *is* so. Aren't you all confused? When you look at yourself honestly, clearly, aren't you all confused? You may be good at science, you may have a good job, but aren't you all asking what it is all about? You are confused and you ask, 'What is your positive remedy, positive action or suggestion regarding this confusion?'

The speaker says there is no suggestion. He is not offering you a *thing*; he is not telling you what to do. But look at this confusion carefully. Don't say there is no confusion. Do you mean to say that when you drive down Bombay you don't see all those hovels, people living there, breeding children? Is that not confusion? Poverty is confusion. Isn't there confusion about gods—the Christian god, the Hindu god? So the speaker says, 'Look at the confusion; don't run away from it.' Then what happens? Where does the confusion begin? Out there or in here? Please answer that question. Where does the confusion lie? Who has created those hovels which you pass by daily? We, human beings, because we have rotten governments, and they allow all that, day after day, year after year. So you realize that you have brought this about, you are responsible for all this. You are responsible for wars because you are a Hindu or a Jew or a Christian. Therefore don't be a Hindu, don't be a Jew, so that you are the whole of humanity. You are a human being, not a label.

Krishnamurti [*reading out*]: *'What is love and how does it arise?'*

Good God! Don't you know what love is? Apparently you don't. Do you love your wife, if you are married? Do you love your children? If you loved your children, would you make them conform to this rotten, immoral society, send them to war to be killed?

First of all, sir, what is love? Can you describe it? Can you put it into words? Or would you find out what is *not* love. Wouldn't you approach it negatively, not positively by saying, 'What's love, tell me how to get it'? When you put this question, do you realize what it implies? That you have never loved anybody, whether you are married, whether you have had sex, or have children. So what is love? Is love jealousy? Is love devotion? Is love possessiveness, domination—the man dominating the woman as he does in this country? Is love attachment? Where there is attachment there is fear. If you are attached to your wife and she turns away from you, you become jealous, angry. So, if one may point out most gently, would you find out what love is by negating what it is not? An ambitious man—like most of you—can never know love; he is concerned only with himself. A man who is devoted to God goes to the temple, mosque, or church, and has tremendous devotion to his guru. But is devotion love? Find out, sir, what it is not. Then you have that perfume, that extraordinary thing. Then life has a meaning—not all your knowledge.

Also, if I may spend two minutes: What is meditation? Why do you meditate? You meditate in order to achieve something, to achieve happiness, peace of mind, illumination, and all that. So your meditation is just like any other person's saying that he is going to become a businessman. Only you call it meditation, the other calls it business, but both want to achieve something. Is that meditation? Or is meditation something entirely different? I won't go into that question now: it is too complicated. But you should look at it—not think about it, but look at it. If you have time, if you have the inclination, if you are interested and if you are serious and concerned with what is happening in the world and to yourself, you have to look at all this. Of course, you are too busy studying and you won't have the time, and therefore you are destroying the world by not looking at your own life and your relationship to the world.

7 February 1984

OTHER BOOKS BY J.KRISHNAMURTI

INTRODUCTION TO THE TEACHINGS

Freedom From the Known
The First and Last Freedom
Beyond Violence
You are the World
Total Freedom - The Essential Krishnamurti
The Book of Life

DAILY LIVING

On Love and Loneliness
On Relationship
On Fear
On Conflict
On Freedom
On Living and Dying
On God

FOR THE YOUNG

Think on These Things
What are You Doing with Your Life?
Life Ahead

FOR PARENTS & EDUCATORS

Education and the Significance of Life
Why are You Being Educated?
School Without Fear
Krishnamurti on Education
Educating the Educator

TALKS AND WRITINGS

Commentaries on Living I, II & III
The Awakening of Intelligence
The Only Revolution
Krishnamurti to Himself
The World Within

BIOGRAPHY

The Life and Death of Krishnamurti
by Mary Lutyens